ARTURO VIVANTE

Writing Fiction

BOSTON

THE WRITER, INC.

PUBLISHERS

Library of Congress Cataloging in Publication Data

Vivante, Arturo.
　　Writing fiction.

　　1. Fiction—Authorship.　I. Title.
PN3355.V5　　　808.3　　　80-11246
ISBN 0-87116-122-2

Printed in the United States of America

CONTENTS

Fiction by
Arturo Vivante

Novels

A GOODLY BABE
DOCTOR GIOVANNI

Collections of short stories

THE FRENCH GIRLS OF KILLINI
ENGLISH STORIES
RUN TO THE WATERFALL

1

WHY WRITE FICTION?

ONE writes fiction in order to know, and for all sorts of other reasons, not the least of which—writers will often say, in jest or in earnest—is to make money. But first of all, and whether they are aware of it or not, in order to know. I think that even in the most frivolous kind of writing there is on the writer's part an urge to know what form the story will take. If there isn't this urge, then there is no art, only an unintelligent rendering. At best, one writes to know something as fully as one possibly can, to reach the core, the secrets that even a familiar situation holds. When an artist draws a sketch of a person, he learns things he didn't know before about that person. It is the same with a writer in his efforts to characterize someone.

Art is always cognitive. While an urge to know seems to me to be of paramount importance, it must be coupled with joy of expression. From such a union good writing is born. Joy of expression is inspiration, imagination at play. The urge to communicate is also important, but not fundamental, for how could one otherwise explain that such great writers as Kafka and Gerard Manley Hopkins wanted their work either to go unpublished or to be destroyed? Perhaps they were content with an audience of one; perhaps their own soul was listener enough for them. Certainly I believe that one good listener, one good reader, makes the story worth telling.

The social function of art is to treat people as individuals and not as categories. Someone who characterizes people according to race, nationality, class, etc., is not a writer in the best sense of the word. Nor should one write about animals and plants as if they were inanimate objects. To regard them as unintelligent is to lose sight of them. And the writer should also impart some of his spirit to places and objects, so that they won't appear to have come out of a mold but to be his very own creations. The moral function of the fiction writer is to write about meaningful things in an original way.

Not always does what comes easiest give the best results. A writer might write verse with great ease and be accused of being facile. The reason could be that verse doesn't provide that particular writer with enough challenge. Sometimes a certain resistance in the material one is working with proves beneficial. Thus, in sculpture, we can picture Michelangelo needing the resistance and hardness of marble, clay being too soft and malleable for him. He believed that the figure he was seeing was imprisoned in the block of marble and that he had to chip away to uncover it, to discover it, to liberate it. Clay wouldn't have worked for him, for clay is usually added rather than subtracted.

Similarly, there are novelists who write huge first drafts only to whittle them down to a few hundred pages, and who consider that trimming the most important part of their work. Dialogue might be conducive to better results than description, and vice versa, depending on the challenge that dialogue and descriptive writing hold for the author. The one-set, few-characters requirement of contemporary theater might stimulate a writer who sees unity and simplicity as a challenge. Bridging time and distance could be the challenge, as in reminiscences, historical novels, or stories set in distant lands or outer space. Challenge is temptation, attraction, fascination. One isn't attracted or fascinated by what is easy to get, right at hand. In every case the form the story will take is the ultimate challenge.

Writing can hardly compete with painting and photography in the detailed description of physical features and color; with music in rendering sound; with the movies in presenting motion; yet—being the most versatile of the arts—writing can do all of these things, and sometimes the very drawbacks it appears to have at first sight can be turned to advantage when they are seen as a challenge. But as far as thought and feelings are concerned, the situation is reversed, and while a painter could give us a very thoughtful portrait, writing, generally speaking, is unparalleled as a medium for expressing thought and feeling. The writer should be aware and take advantage of this. The more thoughtful and thought-provoking a story, the more value it is likely to have. Thus, Chekhov's stories and plays are never sensational; neither are they noted for the amount of physical action in them, but they are extremely thoughtful and provocative.

To say that fiction is dying is to lose sight of the fact that television just can't do what the written word can to express thoughts and feelings.

As writers, we should be aware of what we do best—of our strengths, and of our limitations. Quite often our strength lies in knowing our weaknesses. A writer's limitations can be viewed as his profile; going beyond it, he risks becoming unrecognizable. And yet a writer cannot know his limitations without experimenting tirelessly. He shouldn't be afraid of deepening the same theme, writing many stories about it. A theme has many facets; I, for example, have written three short stories* about an aged man's last days. John Updike in his collection of stories—*Problems*—explores the theme of divorce again and again. It is the same in the other arts. Monet painted water lilies over and over. The subject was much the same, but he deepened his treatment of it with each canvas. It has even been said that a writer has but one theme, which he deepens in each of his stories.

Fiction—especially the novel—is less apt to break with tradition than painting, sculpture, architecture, poetry and music. This is partly because it takes a considerable length of time to read a book, while a person can apprehend the beauty of a painting, a brief poem, or a musical composition in a relatively short span of time. It isn't easy to read

---

* "The Soft Core," *The New Yorker* (June 15, 1972); "The Bell," *The New Yorker* (February 10, 1973); "A Gallery of Women," *The New Yorker* (November 13, 1978).

an abstract book, such as *Finnegans Wake*; an abstract painting, on the other hand, can be seen and admired or disliked in a moment. For this rather simple reason, I think, there is much less abstract narrative than there is abstract art. Also, in writing, the materials are still paper and ink, and the tools pen and typewriter, while in the other arts, all sorts of new materials and instruments have come into use, along with changes in methods and techniques.

Because of the difficulty of appraising fiction, many theories regarding the value of a work of art—for our purposes, a story—have been advanced, held and used by various writers and critics. These theories or criteria may be conveniently classified into four main groups. I think that only the fourth is really valid, but let us examine them one by one:

The first one rests on the idea of imitation of or literal resemblance to life. According to this criterion, a story's value depends on how accurately it reproduces or how close it is to objective reality. A short story by John O'Hara, in which there is a literal rendition of a conversation in a New York bar, comes to mind. This criterion neglects the fact that a story's quality often depends on a sifting of reality to just a few vital touches. Nor does it take into account that a tape recorder and camera may give a complete imitation of objective reality without being necessarily artistic. Imitation requires craftsmanship and patience rather than spontaneity and originality. Such a criterion is therefore inadequate.

The second group rests on the idea of usefulness. According to this theory, a story has to be of some practical use in order to be considered valuable. For a moralist, this

practical purpose is good will, i.e., only a story that enhances good will is of value. Tolstoy, late in life—renoun-
cing some of his earlier work, *War and Peace* in particular—
supported this theory, as he believed that art and good will
at times work at cross purposes. This is the case in stories
about hunting, revenge, war; for example Homer's *Iliad*.
The trouble with this theory is that it makes a story or any
work of art a means to an end, not an end in itself. A story
becomes a tool rather than a creation. While moral issues
do play a part in the intrinsic value of a story, they do so
because truth and beauty are intimately linked, and because an untrue representation of reality would rest on
false premises. But to write a story in order to enhance the
cause of good will would be to relegate and subordinate art
and to impoverish it. Nor would the writer effectively ac-
complish his purpose.

The third group stresses the physical response or reaction
a story will evoke in us. According to this criterion, a story
is of value when it gives the readers pleasure, makes them
laugh or cry, or frightens them. And yet there are stories
that don't exactly give pleasure, since they are sad, and
still not so sad that they will make the readers cry, and
stories not so funny that they will make readers laugh or
not so terrifying that they will make them shudder. There
are stories that will produce none of these physical reac-
tions, but are nevertheless great. James Joyce's *Portrait of the
Artist as a Young Man*, for example, isn't particularly sad or
funny or frightening, but it is a great book.

An extension of this theory holds that a story is worth-
while when it has a pleasing arrangement or plan and when
it has no technical flaws. But F. Scott Fitzgerald's *The Great*

Gatsby has been said to have many defects, yet few will deny its value. This criterion then is also inadequate.

The fourth theory rests on the concept of originality. A story, it holds, is valuable when it is original. Originality has an element of beauty. It is all one with creativity. Only when a work of art is truly original, fresh, new; when it is imaginative, inspired, and shows the creative spark; when the author has put his soul into it, as Melville did in *Moby Dick*, can it be said to be creative. For the reader to identify with the characters and events in such a work of fiction, they need to have a reality of their own. Of the four criteria, I believe this last to be the most valid.

2

WHAT IS A STORY?

A STORY is a quest for life for the writer and for the reader. The story fails if it doesn't have life. There is nothing worse that can be said about a story or a character than that it doesn't come to life.

Life is a story's great source. But life has something which art is glad to do without. Life with its constant needs, its weight, its multiplicity, has a certain rawness, a mass— rugged, rough, irreversible—which is its very power. The writer's role is to refine, to sift. In life one is presented with a clutter of details. In a story one depends on a few touches. It is easy enough to itemize, as in an inventory, the various things in a house. It may be useful, but it will be absolutely unartistic. The writer, to give the quick of life to his description, will tell us what strikes him most, and in a few vivid touches give the whole picture. He is more interested in creating an impression than in trying to be complete. That impression, incidentally, will for our purposes be more complete than a long list of items, for completeness is illusory.

While a story is an impression of life, it is never a copy
of life. A plaster cast of a hand looks and is dead, unartistic, uncreated, because it comes about through a
purely mechanical process, as life never does. In life and in
a story, there are moments that stand out—revelations,
epiphanies—that have something eternal about them, even
though they may pass unnoticed by the public and even-
tually be forgotten. It is as if all time had waited for such a
moment—new and unrepeatable—to happen.

A story doesn't depend upon or lead up to anything that is
outside of itself, as a chapter of a novel may. Essentially, a
story (a whole story, be it a short story or a novel) is not
subordinated or instrumental to anything. It is compact,
self-sustained and self-sufficient. And it has to be new.

Even an ordinary incident, imaginatively described, has
the makings of a story. It would be difficult to write a story
about someone asking you the time of day. Yet, though it
might take the hand of a master, it could be done. It is in
the nature of the artist to find the unusual in the usual, and
the writer would explore all the possibilities that such an
incident might afford. He would welcome the challenge.
The person asking the time might have a disoriented air
that the writer would make capital of. The incident might
be just an excuse to describe a person or two persons, a
portrait. The plot would inevitably be slight, and again the
writer would naturally have an urge to expand, to amplify,
to delve into the characters of the two persons involved.
Letting his fancy roam, he would ask himself not just what
happened but what might have happened, and write it as
though it did happen.

The person, say a young man asked the time of day by a young woman, might answer, "It is time you and I had a cup of coffee together." This would make an ordinary incident into an anecdote. If the young woman agreed and they struck up a friendship, the piece would become a short story. If they got married and had children and grand-children, divorced and later died, it would be a novel, or even two novels or a trilogy.

André Schwartz-Bart's novel *The Last of the Just* spans more than eight centuries, tracing the history of a family to which God has granted one just man in each generation, but the bulk of the book, as the title implies, is about the last member of that family. On the other 'hand, Carson McCullers's short story "A Tree, a Rock, a Cloud," in which a man talks to a boy about love, takes place in just one locale—a café—one morning in less than an hour, or more precisely in about the time it would take to read the story.

There must be much in common between a short story and a play for so many playwrights to have excelled in the short story: Gogol, Chekhov, Oscar Wilde, Pirandello, Somerset Maugham, Tennessee Williams. Perhaps the circumscribed space of a short story, comparable to the limited space of a stage, appealed to them and was like a challenge. It is also interesting to note how well the short story has done in the hands of women. One has only to think of Mary Wilkins Freeman, Katherine Mansfield, Virginia Woolf, Willa Cather, Katherine Anne Porter, Dorothy Parker, Carson McCullers, Eudora Welty, Mary McCarthy, Flannery O'Connor.

A short story, like a flash of lightning, is a vast, all-encompassing moment. One could generalize and say that a novel is more complex, has more characters, and spans more time and space, but this is often not true, nor is the inverse always true of a short story. Joyce's *Ulysses* takes place in a day. So do Virginia Woolf's *Mrs. Dalloway*, Saul Bellow's *Seize the Day*, and Aleksandr Solzhenitsyn's *One Day in the Life of Ivan Denisovich*. It would be hard to write about the whole of a person's life in a short story. It may cover a lifetime, but it concentrates on a certain aspect of that life. I wrote a short story about a parish priest* whose one wish was to be buried in his own cemetery, and of how it was denied him. I did write something about his life—for the reader had to know him in order to care about him—but no more than needed to make his wish and its denial relevant, poignant. To have written more would have altered the scope of the story, would have thrown the story out of focus.

Not only does a short story have a different length, it also has a different pace from a novel. A novel is the sustained flight of geese from Labrador to Florida, a short story, the flight of a sparrow across a fence, from field to field.

Articles are all too often a mass of information. Not so short stories. They, too, will provide some information, but they can only carry so much. A short story can't be exactly defined or confined. Like a cloud it cannot be put into a box or towed. "The magic hand of chance" has a part in its shaping. Whatever a short story is, it is never a list or a summary. And this, of course, applies also to a novel or any work of art.

---

* "The Parish Priest," published in *Anon* 1974, *Eighth Annual Anthology of Fiction and Poetry* (Street Fiction Press).

Observation, perception play a fundamental role. Ideas
spring from them, at any time—often while the writer isn't
at his desk. He might be reading a book, seeing a movie,
or listening to a conversation. He not only observes the
situation, but he wonders what turns it might take, and
often this—this flight of the imagination—forms the basis
of his story. Thus, I was once in a third-class compartment
of an Italian train. There were eight other passengers, including a baby in his mother's arms and an old man with a
beard who reminded me of Santa Claus. Nothing much
happened, but in my mind something did, and I wrote it
out as a story.* The old man, when a steward comes in
with a trayful of candies, fruit, cookies, drinks and a
thermos of coffee, buys more than he can afford and hands
everyone things. The compartment becomes like a room
with a party given by the old man with the beard. Then the
ticket collector comes in. The old man can't find his ticket,
nor does he have enough money to buy a new one. He has
to leave the train at the next station. The only one who
does anything for him is the baby who reaches out with his
lollipop to him.

The writer must have an open mind; he must be willing
to be sidetracked. If he too determinedly pursues one single
objective, he might miss a more fruitful one. In this he
resembles a scientist—Fleming, for example, who, while
conducting an experiment on something else, found that a
mold that had settled on his agar plate destroyed the germs
he was working on. Impressed by this, he left his experiment to pursue this new thing, penicillin. The writer, when

* "The Old Man with the Beard," *The New Yorker* (April 4, 1959).

he has an idea, usually makes a note of it, and if a beautiful line comes to his mind, he writes it down, because he
knows that original ideas don't knock twice, that if they
are forgotten it is hard to think of them again, and that a
thought well expressed is precious and rare and often the
cornerstone for a story. He also knows that if he ignores the
beckoning muse she will not visit him again as she used to.

One cannot stress enough that a story ought to be suggestive: what is left out is often as important as what is put
in. There is nothing that the reader hates to be told as
much as the obvious. He doesn't like to be led all the way
as though there were something wrong with him. He likes
to bridge certain gaps by himself. In one of the first short
stories I wrote, called "The Snake*," a boy, spending his
vacation with his mother in a house by the sea, in Italy,
during the summer drought, has to go and fetch water at a
spring every day. Halfway back he pauses at a trough-like
rock in his path and some water spills from his two full
pails. As he resumes walking, he looks back and sees a
snake drinking the water. This happens each day. And a
certain attachment develops between him and the snake.
Then, toward the end of August, his father comes to pick
him and his mother up to take them home. He worries
about the thirsty snake. But that last night a rainstorm
breaks the drought, and where there was a stone there's a
puddle. The story ends on that note. If I had gone on to
explain that the snake now had plenty of water, it would
have been an insult to the reader's intelligence. Even in a
children's book such an explanation is best omitted.

---

* "The Snake," *The Manchester Guardian* (December 1, 1955).

Again, in a factual account that had the form of a short
story, the Russian poet Yevtushenko tells of meeting Robert
Kennedy at a party at the Kennedys' during the 1968
primaries. He asks Robert why he wants to run for President, and Robert replies that he wishes to continue his
brother's work. Yevtushenko suggests they drink to Robert's
victory, but cautions that in Russia for the wish to come true
they must throw and break the glasses. Robert looks at the
precious glasses and says he had better ask his wife. She
brings two new glasses of champagne. They drink and throw
the glasses away, but they don't break. They are made of
plastic. A sense of doom, a presentiment of evil comes over
the guest as he and Kennedy look at one another. The article
rightly ends there. If it continued, to say that Robert
Kennedy shortly thereafter was killed, the effect would be
weakened.

Writing is a quest for knowledge. The very word story
comes from the Greek "to know." The mere exercise of
writing is valuable; it is conducive to knowledge; it leads
one toward the unfolding of the tale; it anchors thoughts
which might otherwise drift and be lost; it sets them in
place so that one can build on them or from them; it helps
one think; it is very close to thinking, but one short step
removed. Writing indeed requires very little physical
action; it is the tracing of our thoughts.

If one has a good idea, then an urge to express it, to
write it, comes over one, and that urge keeps the writer at
his desk. He is curious to know what form that idea will
take. He acquires a certain working rhythm which he is
loath either to interrupt or to abandon. If he doesn't keep
at it, the idea may be a weak one. If the idea is a com-

pelling one, the writer may not have the problem of finding
the time to write it so much as the problem of finding the
time to do anything else. But there is no setting up of rules.
There are writers who write steadily every day, and others
who need to spend a great deal of time doing nothing
before they can do anything: They may not write for
many days—then they enter into a feverish spell of activity
that lasts till they are almost exhausted, when again they
fall into a long period of repose.

At times, while writing, the telling of the story seems all
that matters; at other times the story seems just an excuse
to describe characters, their feelings, their thoughts. But
obviously the two sides are inextricably bound, nor could
one exist without the other. Like any living organism, a
story is spoiled if it is taken apart and divided.

3

CHARACTERIZATION

IN A LETTER to a woman who complained that she couldn't see his characters, D.H. Lawrence said that his weren't "Kodak characterizations." He meant, of course, that he wasn't interested in a photographic or literal representation of people. Passport characterizations—weight, height, color of eyes, of hair, complexion, scars, date and place of birth—or, worse still, FBI characterizations like those pinned on post office bulletin boards, are the antithesis of art, and the writer would do well to avoid them. Characterizations of that sort are a useful tool, but art is not a tool; it is an end in itself, self-sustaining, and not—to quote Lawrence again—"a tedious link in the chain of cause and effect."

Indeed, a description of things that the person can do something about—clothes, hair, eyeglasses, make-up—may tell more than an account of something he can't alter, like the shape of his chin. To give an example, I might write: "One of the guests was a lanky, spectacled Frenchman in plus fours, with the energy of an electric eel.'' For our purposes, it is more accurate to describe the person as "lanky" than to say that he is six feet tall and weighs 140 pounds. The rest is an attempt to characterize the person as dynamic. The glasses may even seem to be flashing, though this isn't said. Or I might write: "The girl peeked into the room. She wore eye shadow and looked as if she wore a mask, like a raccoon. As she came in she seemed a model straight from Paris. Everyone smelled her perfume—subtle, expensive.'' Again, things she wears, things she can do something about, things that tell of her taste.

A woman who dyes her hair red, wears rouge and red lipstick, and paints her nails red might be expressing the fire that is in her. She might, on the other hand, be trying to make up for what she conceives her nature is lacking. In either case such a description would help a writer get his point across.

Willa Cather, to characterize Paul, in the first paragraph of her short story "Paul's Case," makes much of what he wears:

> His clothes were a trifle outgrown, and the tan velvet on the collar of his open overcoat was frayed and worn; but for all that there was something of the dandy about him, and he wore an opal pin in his neatly knotted black four-in-hand, and a red carnation in his buttonhole.

Even so, the characterizations just made are relatively exterior ones. What we need are inward characterizations—characterizing people by how and by what they feel, think, say, do. In that order probably. So in "Paul's Case," Willa Cather, deepening Paul's characterization, writes that the teachers' aversion for him:

lay in a sort of hysterically defiant manner of the boy's; in the contempt which they all knew he felt for them, and which he seemingly made not the least effort to conceal.

Nancy Hale in her short story "Midsummer" characterizes a passionate sixteen-year-old girl by describing her feelings:

> She could not imagine what was happening to her; she had never imagined such violent sensations as beat at her; inside she was like the summer itself—sultry and fiery, and racked by instantaneous thunderstorms.

In a short story of mine entitled "The Stream"* and written in the first person, about a seventeen-year-old boy just released from internment, I say:

> I felt like a child who has been long in bed with a fever and finds that on getting up his legs are too shaky for him to go skipping around as he wanted . . . Wholly unaccustomed to freedom, like a bird just set free from a cage, I found that the beautiful, long flights I had dreamed couldn't be quite as readily accomplished as they had been in my dreams.

Alan Sillitoe in his short story "The Loneliness of the Long Distance Runner," about a young man who, to assert his individuality, purposely loses a cross-country race, reveals the protagonist's character by disclosing his thoughts and by what he says to himself:

> I'll lose that race because I'm not a race horse at all.

Joan Didion, in her novel *Play It As It Lays*, describes Maria's distraught state of mind by relating her thoughts,

---

* *The New Yorker* (August 25, 1958).

questions, and imaginings, and in this way effectively
characterizes her as a woman in a crisis, torn by remorse:

> She was consumed that year by questions. Exactly what
> time had it happened, precisely what had she been doing in
> New York at the instant her mother lost control of the car
> outside Tonopah. What was her mother wearing, thinking.
> What was she doing in Tonopah anyway. She imagined her
> mother having a doctor's appointment in Tonopah, and the
> doctor saying cancer, and her mother cracking up the car on
> purpose . . . Maria did not know whether any of that had
> actually happened, but she used to think it, used to think it
> particularly around the time the sun set in New York, think
> about her mother dying in the desert light, the daughter un-
> available in the eastern dark.

What someone says to oneself and what one thinks are so
close they are almost the same thing, except that sometimes
a person thinks in images rather than in words. Dorothy
Parker's story "A Telephone Call" is written out entirely
as a soliloquy—what the protagonist is saying to herself.
Her features aren't described—we certainly don't get a
photographic description of her—but we see her and get to
know her very clearly nevertheless. Here is the beginning
of the story:

> Please God, let him telephone me now. Dear God, let him
> call me now. I won't ask anything else of You, truly I won't.
> It isn't very much to ask. It would be so little to You, God,
> such a little, little thing. Only let him telephone now. Please
> God. Please, please, please.

In her short story "Everything That Rises Must Con-
verge," Flannery O'Connor, through a few descriptive
touches and dialogue and action, characterizes a proud,

resentful, angry black woman whose child has been offered
a penny by a white woman:

> The huge woman turned and for a moment stood, her
> shoulders lifted and her face frozen with frustrated rage, and
> stared at Julian's mother. Then all at once she seemed to ex-
> plode like a piece of machinery that had been given one ounce
> of pressure too much. Julian saw the black fist swing out with
> the red pocketbook. He shut his eyes and cringed as he heard
> the woman shout, "He don't take nobody's pennies!" When
> he opened his eyes, the woman was disappearing down the
> street with the little boy staring wide-eyed over her shoulder.
> Julian's mother was sitting on the sidewalk.

Stephen Dixon, in his 1977 O. Henry Award-winning
story entitled "Mac in Love," uses dialogue and some
action without describing the physical features of the protagonist, to characterize him as a young man in love who
won't take no for an answer. As with Dorothy Parker, a
few lines suffice to give the picture:

> She said "You're crazy, Mac," and shut the door. I
> knocked. She said "Leave me be?" I rang the bell. She said
> "Please don't make a fuss." I kicked the door bottom. She
> said "Mac, the neighbors. You'll get the police here and me
> thrown out." I said "Then let me in." She said "Maybe some
> other day." I said "Just for a minute to explain." She said
> "There's nothing to explain. The incident's over. It never
> should've begun."

Prince Mishkin, in Dostoevsky's novel *The Idiot*, is introduced with a description of his physical features, but we
don't really get to know him until we *hear* him. He is in a
third-class railroad carriage returning to St. Petersburg
after two years as a patient in Switzerland, and though the

questions put to him by his fellow passengers are often im-
pertinent and inappropriate, he doesn't mind answering
them all. "The money you must have wasted on those
doctors," one says to him, and another adds, "Those
foreigners are sure out to fleece us." And Mishkin replies
gently, "Oh, but you are quite wrong in my case. My
doctor paid for my fare back, even though he had very little
money, and he kept me there at his expense." He is anything but a cynic, but if he were characterized by such a
statement—i.e., that he wasn't a cynic—it wouldn't be
memorable; it would be just a bit of information, not a
characterization, not a presentation.

I am not saying that one shouldn't write about the physical features of people—quite the contrary; but they should
be described in their essence. "So cold, so fresh, so sea-
clear her face was, it was like kissing a flower that grows
near the surf," writes Lawrence in *Women in Love*, and in
another passage, "It was in the curves of his brows and his
chin, rich, fine, exquisite curves, the powerful beauty of
life itself. She could not say what it was, but there was a
sense of richness and of liberty."

One may write about the color of the eyes, say that they
were blue, and run the risk—as in a poor painting—of not
transfiguring inert pigment into live color. To make it live,
to make that a live, created, essential blue, one has to do
more—to tell about the light of those eyes, their expression,
the way they look, what they see, how they see it, and tell
it in an original way. You might say, "He looked at her
longingly, desirously," and you might not be saying much,
because it isn't very original. Or you might say, "He
looked at her as if he were trying to draw from the visual

connection more than it could ever concede,'' and be saying something more—more memorable, more incisive—
because it's more original.

Characterization frequently depends on the use of the
right word. Here is a passage from a short story of mine
entitled ''Adria,''* about a live-in maid who takes care of a
prosperous old widower in a house in which his family also
lives:

> The truth was Adria was better company—a woman of a
> richer nature—than his sallow daughter, or, for that matter,
> anyone else in the house, and now that he didn't go out so
> much it was essential to have a sassy, handsome woman in his
> reach.

I think that the word ''sassy,'' especially when contrasted with ''sallow,'' is accurate, appropriate, and, more
effectively than any other word used in the story, characterizes the live-in maid.

In J.D. Salinger's short story ''For Esmé—with Love
and Squalor,'' the word ''extremely'' is spoken again and
again by Esmé, a child who wants to sound sophisticated.

Jean Rhys, in her novel *Quartet*, writes about the protagonist:

> Her long eyes slanted upwards towards the temples and
> were gentle and oddly remote in expression.

I think the first part of this sentence characterizes her less
effectively than the second part—the second part is original
and inward, the first part fairly commonplace and exterior.

---

* *The New Yorker* (March 8, 1969).

Though adjectives are often essential, a fiction writer shouldn't indulge in using them to state the qualities of a character. Thus it would be less effective to say that someone is "stingy" than to have an episode in which that person won't lend money to a friend in need. The latter approach characterizes the person through action or inaction and is much more likely to create an impression on the reader.

But most important of all, I think, a character is well described, is a really living character, when readers are made to feel that they know him well and still want to know more about him. This may sound like a paradox, but the moment readers feel that they know him sufficiently, that they know him well enough, that they don't need or want to know anything more about him, then that character becomes uninteresting and dead—in life and in fiction. The moment readers cease to wonder about something, they stop loving it. A reader should want to know the character infinitely.

Though the writer may tell all he possibly can about the characters, though he may spare nothing, keep no secrets, there should still be some mystery left in them at the end of the story, so that the reader will wonder about them, and they will live on and on in his mind, long after the book is closed.

No matter how intimately you know a character, he should still have something of the stranger in him, to goad your curiosity through the pages, and beyond them.

The choice of suitable proper names for fictional characters is an art and often is a good measure of a writer's skill. A name like Ethan Frome is original and somehow very appropriate for the protagonist of Edith Wharton's novel by the same name. Besides suiting the character, the name has a certain assonance that makes it attractive. And being biblical, Ethan is a likely name for a New Englander.

Two similar names for two characters in the same story or novel—like Lisa and Lina—ought to be avoided so there will be no confusion in the reader's mind. Naming a person of great physical strength Leo or Samson, or a cautious one Prudence, is too obvious, deliberate, and old-fashioned. Dickens often made up names to give the reader an insight into their character: Skimpole, Pecksniff, Squeers, Gradgrind, Swiveller. Fiction writers don't often do it now, but Ken Kesey in his novel *One Flew Over the Cuckoo's Nest* calls the dreadful nurse Miss Ratched.

A writer intent on plot may learn from the way flashbacks are handled in the movies; a writer intent on characterization may learn from a study of close-ups in films. A face in a close-up is bigger than life-size; the writer might imagine it so in his fiction too and focus on the various details to advantage—describe the eyes, for instance, as if he were viewing them through an enlargement lens: "Her face appeared immense to him, as in a close-up. He could see the blood vessels in the whites of her eyes, angry, like streaks of lightning that would not fade, and in her pupils he could see himself, surprised, astonished, fearful."

Just as a person's character in life is disclosed throughout life's duration, so in a work of fiction the characters disclose themselves throughout the book and not just when they are introduced.

Some writers claim that they start their stories and novels by thinking of certain characters and then building a plot around them or fitting a plot to them. Others say that they first think of a plot and then fit the characters to it. Most writers, however—and it has certainly been my experience—won't make such a neat division or distinction between character and plot. I cannot think of one without the other, nor would I be able to start a story without some inkling of both in my mind. It has been said that a person's character is his fate, and since fate and plot could be taken as synonyms, we could say that the story's characters are its plot. It has also been said that a character can't be altogether invented or made from scratch, that is, with no prototype or—since many characters in fiction are composites—prototypes in mind. In writing my stories, I surely use people I have known or met or seen, however briefly. In fact, I can think of only one case in which I did not have a real person in mind: when I wrote "The Honeymoon,"* a story about a young shepherd and his bride who leave their remote mountain village and for the first time in their lives travel to a big city for their honeymoon. In this instance, I find it impossible to say that I drew from anyone I knew or met or saw or read about. Only the mountain was real. Of course, it is entirely possible that even in this case I might—without being aware of it—have drawn from people who crossed my path so briefly as to have been later forgotten.

I once read in *The New Yorker* a short story that was a character sketch with little or no plot. Though the characters seemed very true to me I thought it was pointless and I

---

* From *The Best American Short Stories of 1974*, Edited by Martha Foley (Houghton Mifflin)

told my editor so. "But if the characters seemed very true then that was the point," the editor said, and of course she was right.

An important question arises: does a writer need to have a hard edge to write effectively about a brutal villain and his crimes? The question is intriguing. The writer loses his identity and becomes the character he is portraying; in his mind he commits those dreadful deeds, utters those fearful words, and writes them—which is more than imagining them. While he is at it, there is no room for kindness in his heart.

The writer partakes of the life of his characters. Dostoevsky wrote about this in his novel *The Insulted and the Injured:*

> If ever I've been happy, it hasn't been during the first moments of elation over my successes, but when I had neither read nor shown my work to anyone, during those long nights passed amid my dreams and enthusiastic hopes, when, working with a passion, I lived with the characters I had created, as though they were my parents and people who really existed; I loved them, I partook of their joy and of their sadness, and on occasion I have shed some real tears over the lack of judgment of one of my heroes.

There are writers like Dickens, Balzac, Dostoevsky who had a genius for creating one original character after another and for giving each character such an imprint that in talking of a real person, someone may compare him to one of these invented characters, and say, "He is a Dostoevsky character," or, "He is a character out of Balzac," "Out of Dickens." This is quite an achievement.

It means that the author succeeded in creating a little world of his own, peopled with a set of characters all his own, unstylized, distinct with his own personality, always recognizable, unmistakable. One cannot say this of many writers. In America perhaps the only living one who has achieved this is Tennessee Williams. It isn't unusual for people to say, "A Tennessee Williams character," "A character out of a play or story of Tennessee Williams." Such characters assume an uncanny reality; Balzac, on his deathbed, was angry with those around him because they wouldn't get him Bianchon, a doctor who only existed in his novels. "I want Dr. Bianchon," he kept saying, but Dr. Bianchon was to be found only in the pages of his books. Such characters become almost more real than those that nature has made.

There are some critics who classify characters into "round" and "flat," terms hardly better than the "soft" and "hard" which some use for poetry—and ought to reserve for drinks. More to the point, it seems to me, would be to divide characters into consistent and inconsistent ones. No writer, however bold, would dare mix into any of his characters traits so incompatible as God dares mix into a man. Nevertheless, a good writer, to make his characters lifelike, will infuse a certain amount of inconsistency into them, for an absolutely consistent, one-sided character is unnatural, unlifelike, uncreated, mechanical and unconvincing. How inconsistent, and still how plausible, a writer's characters are may be a measure of his skill.

4

DIALOGUE

T O BE successful, conversation depends on something so interesting being said that it will draw attention and evoke a response or a comment. It will also depend on an atmosphere being engendered in which the timid lose their shyness, the bold find their match, and truth is like a Ping-Pong ball balanced on a jet of water and rolling, rolling, while everyone aspires to send it higher. These qualities also apply to dialogue, which may be defined as conversation in a work of fiction. There should be a nexus, link, or connection between one line and another. The dialogue should make a point. The gist of it, its purport, should come through.

In writing dialogue, the writer needs a good ear for everyday speech and for the voice of literature. As long as he can sound natural and convincing and not stilted, he shouldn't be afraid of letting the dialogue rise to the highest pinnacle of eloquence he can achieve. Eloquence, as a matter of fact, is never stilted. The author cannot but break with the ordinary, the mediocre, the dull. He may give an interesting and amusing rendition of the pompous, as Jane Austen does in certain pages of *Pride and Prejudice*, but can one reenact the boring? Unless he wants to characterize a person as such, the writer should avoid the formal, the complex, which, if reprehensible in descriptive writing, are even more so in dialogue. He should also shun the triteness, repetitiousness and clumsiness of everyday speech but should retain its freshness, pliancy, and naturalness.

The following excerpt from my story "Angels in the Air"* has the tone of everyday speech and advances the story by giving it direction and holding it to a certain course. Also, I present both points of view and try to make them as convincing as possible by identifying first with one character, then with the other:

> "I don't think I'd want to go to Spain with all those bullrings," a young American said, just back from Greece.
> "Oh, I think bullfighting's a thrilling spectacle," an American lady said.
> "Do you?" Mildred said. "I can't get a thrill out of an animal's pain."
> "It's the courage that's thrilling, not the pain," Priscilla said.
> "Well, I don't much admire that kind of courage, and I certainly can't ignore the pain," Mildred said, looking at Priscilla with surprise.
> "But the bull would be killed anyway, and in a more cowardly way—slaughtered. They are, you know, everywhere," the American lady said.

---

* "Angels in the Air," *The New Yorker* (June 25, 1966).

"For food, though. Not for fun. I don't think killing should be a form of entertainment," Mildred said.

"Oh, what's the difference?" Priscilla said.

"I think there is a difference. Our whole civilization is based on drawing distinctions, though they may be very subtle."

The two girls looked at one another as if aware for the first time of a discord or difference between them.

Through dialogue, the writer can at the same time express his opinions and characterize people. In this story, set in a house in which all sorts of moral and political questions are aired, Priscilla and Mildred—old friends who on their trip talked mainly about the scenery, cars, other drivers, the knots and hitches of the day and the weather—get to know each other even too well, and part company.

Just as passport characterizations are to be avoided, so is passport dialogue—Where were you born? How old are you? What is your profession? Address?—except in the mouths of officials. Dialogue ought to have the quick of life. The subject broached should be one that the reader can identify with. The characters should soon come to the core of the question. Short stories and novels often open with dialogue. This should not just serve as an appetizer, but should be the first bite of the main course. In a short story of mine called "At the Dinner Table,"* husband and wife are expecting some guests for dinner, and the husband doesn't want his old, invalid father to be at the table. The story opens:

"I thought we were going to be eight," Giacomo said to his wife, Jessie, seeing that she was setting the table for nine.

---

* *The New Yorker* (December 30, 1974).

"Your father," she said.

"Do you really want him to sit with us tonight?"

"Yes, why not? He enjoys a little company."

"I know he enjoys it, but it's embarrassing. He's much better off in his room."

"No, he isn't," she said, and went on setting the table.

"I just hope he doesn't get one of those sneezing attacks. He doesn't know enough to leave the table. And then sometimes he just looks down, his chin against his chest, in a kind of stupor."

"Oh, not a stupor. Don't make things seem worse than they are. You should talk to him more."

"I think he should stay in bed. He dishes out his food to whoever's sitting next to him."

"A lot of people do that."

"And he keeps saying the same things all the time."

"So do you," she said, and laughed. "Try to be a little cheerful."

The story goes on to show that the father's presence actually saves what might otherwise have been a very dull evening.

What a character says should be distinct, should differ from what someone else says, enough to identify him or her immediately and to make it unnecessary for the writer to tell who is speaking. There should, in other words, always be a certain contrast between the speech of fictional characters. Even when people are agreeing, the way they speak and what they say should, ideally, serve to make them recognizable. Good dialogue speaks for itself and doesn't often need descriptive passages or tag lines to modify it, qualify it, and explain it. Whenever there is some doubt as to who is saying what, a name or a pronoun should be supplied, for clarity is not expendable. Instead of using "he said," or "she said," some fiction writers prefer such expressions as, "he observed," "he put in," "he offered," "he exclaimed," but this style is rather old-fashioned. As much as possible, the speeches should carry the voice, the personality of the character who is speaking. Sometimes, in an effort to identify with the character speaking, the writer will try to imitate the character's voice, inflections, and facial expression.

Just as a sketch of a place will make a lengthy description unnecessary, so dialogue is often a shortcut to characterization, to gaining insight into the situation, to expressing the author's philosophy or theme, to contrasting two points of view and to the conflict of the story. In Nabokov's novel *Lolita*, for example, we learn of Lolita's mother's death through a telephone call: "Mrs. Humbert, sir, has been run over and you'd better come quick." Her death takes place offstage, as in ancient Greek drama. A lengthy, detailed, and difficult description is thus avoided. That line of dialogue is, in other words, a shortcut.

Much of the characterization of Phoenix Jackson in Eudora Welty's short story "A Worn Path," and the climax of the story, are in dialogue. Phoenix, a poor, frail, very old lady, walks a long way from the country into town to buy some medicine for her grandson, only to forget, in the dispensary, what she has come for:

> "Now, how is the boy?" asked the nurse.
> Old Phoenix did not speak.
> "I said, how is the boy?"
> But Phoenix only waited and stared straight ahead, her face very solemn and withdrawn into rigidity . . . . . .
> "He isn't dead, is he?"

At last there came a flicker and then a flame of comprehension across her face, and she spoke.

"My grandson. It was my memory had left me. There I sat and forgot why I made my long trip."

"Forgot?" The nurse frowned. "After you came so far?"

When people are arguing, the dialogue tends to be short-clipped and fast. Often one character interrupts the other, and when this happens, a dash is supplied after the last word spoken by the person who has been interrupted. On the other hand, when the dialogue is leisurely, philosophical, descriptive, the exchanges tend to be longer. In modern fiction one rarely reads the drawn-out speeches or lectures that were so common in nineteenth-century fiction. A fiction writer must avoid didactic writing, especially didactic dialogue. This may be preachy, moralistic prose, or expository prose that usually denotes the intrusion of the writer coming in at the wrong time, in the wrong way, to explain something that should have been explained earlier in the narrative in some other fashion. James Agee, reviewing the film *Casablanca*, quotes the wife's plea to her husband, "Oh, Victor, please don't go to the underground meeting tonight," as an example of expository writing; in real life she would merely have said. "Please don't go!" or simply, "Don't go!"

Usually, except in brief flashbacks, each speaker is given a separate paragraph, and the modifiers and qualifiers of the spoken lines are put within that paragraph.

Soliloquies—what one says to oneself—which, unlike thoughts, are put within quotes, can be viewed as dialogue when the ideas expressed are in opposition to each other: "Why not? You are a fool to do it. No, I am not." As in life, so in fiction, one's emotions—love, hate, etc.—come best to the fore in dialogue. And dialogue is the best vehicle for humor.

Through dialogue, we come to know a character directly, with immediacy. We hear him. He is given a voice. Dialogue can also be used by the fiction writer to describe characters other than those who are speaking. Lee Zacharias, at the beginning of her short story "Helping Muriel Make It Through the Night,"* about a woman who has been left by her husband, has several people talking. Not only do they characterize themselves—they also describe others, present and absent, and in this way the situation is soon brought into focus. Certainly readers are attracted by dialogue, for it is perhaps closer to life than anything else is in fiction.

---

* *Intro 8: The Liar's Craft*, edited by George Garrett (Doubleday)

5

PLOT

TWO or more traits or characters or threads meeting, weaving into a knot, a tight spot, then something, someone undoing the knot, bringing about some kind of solution, resolution, dénouement—this, I think, is what most people mean by plot. But such a definition of plot is acceptable only if we are willing to admit that all sorts of contradictions, incompatible traits, inconsistencies, exist and interplay even in the mind of one person alone, and that this interplay, as in a character sketch, can also be understood as plot. In French, the word for it is *trame*, a weave, or *intrigue*, and some kind of complication is inherent in it.

Unless we are dealing with the absurd (as in the Theater of the Absurd), a plot should be (1) plausible and (2) unpredictable. "Original" is a more comprehensive term than "unpredictable." Anything original is necessarily unpredictable. The reverse is not quite true: what is unpredictable isn't necessarily original. Originality carries with it an element of beauty. Not so unpredictability, or, for that matter, eccentricity. Yet the term unpredictable, though limited, is a useful one. It gives us something to work with. Certainly, plausibility by itself isn't sufficient. An ordinary laundry list is plausible and convincing enough; a commonplace schedule is plausible, or a paltry account of what one did on a particular day. But since they are predictable they are uninteresting. Make that laundry list, that schedule, that account, very unusual, i.e. unpredictable, original, and they become interesting. Unpredictability by itself is also insufficient. For if the plot or story isn't plausible, if we don't believe it, it will fall flat, it won't carry us along with it.

A plot should have a certain simplicity if it is to hold our attention. We should be able to understand it. We soon lose interest in a plot that is hard to follow. Simplicity has a power that one is apt to underestimate. It is clarity. It is pureness. It is the full, rich, active silence that Mozart knew and wrote about in his letters. It is the stillness of a Giotto or Piero della Francesca painting. The contemplation in a Raphael or a Perugino. The concentration of a play of Sophocles. The wide embracing quality of love in the Bible. The vastness of Einstein's $E = mc^2$. It has a spellbinding quality. It is full of implications and very suggestive. It lends wonder to the story.

What is awkward, gauche, is also often wrong. James D. Watson, as he says in his book *The Double Helix*, knew he had come upon the right structure of the molecule of DNA when he saw that it looked "pretty." He could have said elegant, but pretty is a better word—simpler. The relationship between truth and beauty of expression is one of the most intriguing, mysterious and wonderful aspects of art.

Sometimes a plot, though extraordinary and almost incredible things happen in it, becomes plausible, convincing, credible, because of the intensity of the writing. In Ken Kesey's remarkable novel *One Flew Over the Cuckoo's Nest*, the Chief's exploits at the end—his mercy killing, his lifting the massive counter, hurling it against the reinforced window and making his escape—would, except for the intensity of the writing, appear unbelievable.

It is often said that in a plot, in a story, there must be conflict. Now conflict seems to me too strong a word. Would it not be sufficient for a story to have contrast? Contrast seems the more useful, the more generally applicable of the two terms. If there's conflict in a story so much the better, but contrast will make a story too. In my story "The Lighthouse,"* a young boy visits an old lighthouse keeper. There is no conflict in the story that I can see; there is contrast between youth and old age, sickness and health, a good memory and forgetfulness. But no conflict, or at least nothing that I would call conflict.

A plot should have a sense of causality and purpose. The actions—and by actions I also mean thoughts, feelings— should be justified, rooted in experience, lived through, suffered or enjoyed, if they are to be convincing. The reader or listener constantly asks why; he wants to know the reason for that action, for that thought. Just as in life he wants to know. He hates to be lost, to be disoriented. If there is no reason for the action, the reader wants to know why. The character may have to be explained more fully or

---

* *The New Yorker* (January 20, 1968).

the theme, the underlying concept, may have to be deepened. And why purpose? Because otherwise the story doesn't go anywhere; it has no forward movement, no drive. That is, again, unless the writer doesn't want it to go anywhere. But, if that is his point, it should be made clear. The cause lies in the past; the goal or purpose in the future. Something vaguely surmised or suspected, mysterious, in the future, is the basis of suspense. It is that something that entices the reader, that stimulates his curiosity, that makes him turn the pages and read every line. Some inkling, some intimation of what is to come, some allusion, some promise of future development, if subtly suggested, will help that forward momentum. It is the same in our lives—we need something to look forward to if we are not to become bored and depressed.

That promise of future development may be inherent in the title of a novel or short story, as in Willa Cather's *Death Comes for the Archbishop,* or in any number of titles with the word "mystery" in them. It may also be found in the first few lines of a work of fiction, as in my short story called "The Diagnostician,"* which begins, " 'Oh, my God,' he heard his wife say in the other room." More often it's used at the end of a chapter, where it serves as a "hook" to carry the reader into the next chapter and keep him from putting the book down. A chapter may end, for example, with someone getting lost in a marshy bog. The reader, if he cares about the character (and that's one of the reasons characterization is so important), will feel compelled to turn to the next chapter to know what is going to happen.

* *The New Yorker* (December 5, 1970).

Such a device is what saved Scheherazade in the *Arabian Nights*. Suspense will also often depend on observing a strict chronological sequence.

Like a river in flood, gaining strength from all of its tributaries, a good story should build up as it goes. And this is perhaps the hardest thing to achieve. It involves strength; it requires control. Writer—and reader—have the feeling of being carried away with the flood. Yet the writer must be abreast of it, neither behind it nor ahead of it. He is the originator but there comes a point when the characters seem to move by themselves, and the writer's work has assumed a life of its own—a life that is ever in danger of failing or being distorted. The writer must do nothing artificial to it, lest it lose that spontaneity which is the chief quality of life and of art.

In Ernest Hemingway's *The Old Man and the Sea*, the old man, a fisherman, ends up with nothing, an outcome which, though it is in line with Hemingway's pessimism, doesn't prevent him and his hero from striving for something with all the strength they are capable of. It is this contrast between aspiration and achievement that makes the writing so poignant.

Too neat a plot is unlifelike, contrived, unconvincing. Life just isn't like that, isn't that neat and well ordered. It is in fact rather disordered, confused, frequently a mess, and we try to find rhyme or reason in it and often fail.

Joan Didion's novel *Play It As It Lays* reflects just such a life. At the beginning and at the end of her novel, Maria is in a hospital under treatment for a nervous breakdown. In between lies what led up to that breakdown. Skillfully, in terse, crisp prose, often in dialogue, Didion takes us back and forth through Maria's life—her mother's death in a car crash, an abortion, a sick child, a friend's suicide, flash before us in quick succession, through very short chapters. Maria's sense of failure and at the same time her intense, passionate, almost heroic efforts to find some way out of the confusion, some path that will lead her to sanity, away from the abyss, and let her see things more clearly, hold the novel together, provide the unifying thread.

The unifying thread in Elizabeth Hardwick's introspective novel *Sleepless Nights*, told in the first person, is compassion woven with affection. The narrator's parents, friends, New York intellectuals, a Dutch doctor, a cleaning woman and others are remembered in what certainly isn't a conventional plot but rather an artful melange of reminiscences, entries, letters, character sketches, landscapes.

As Robert Kiely points out in his review of Susan Cheever's novel *Looking for Work*, many contemporary novels seem to follow the pace and techniques of movies: scene follows scene rapidly, abruptly, with many flashbacks, and with close-ups and distant views alternating. Continuity isn't their strong point.

More in the traditions of the nineteenth century are most of the novels of Iris Murdoch; *The Unicorn*, for example, is written in a step-by-step, compelling, suspenseful, chronological sequence. In it a young woman goes to be the companion of Hannah, a unique, mysterious enchantress who is held almost in thralldom in a lonely mansion in the north of England.

Again, in John Fowles' *The French Lieutenant's Woman*, a novel about conflicts of love, there is what might be called a strong traditional plot. At the close of it, however, the author, obviously unable to find the right ending, offers alternative ones, in what, at least to me, seems an unsatisfying solution.

Just as too neat a plot is unlifelike, contrived and unconvincing, so also a plot that is too sensational has these defects. It is melodramatic rather than dramatic, catering to effect rather than dictated by cause.

In John Cheever's novel *Falconer* there is a strong theme—freedom, a convict's yearning to escape. He is in prison right at the beginning of the novel. Why he is there is made clear later, through deftly inserted flashbacks. As the novel develops it broadens—we get to know his wife, other inmates, the brother he has killed, the conditions within the jail, his loves, his past, his present, his despair and his hopes. They all complement one another. And at the end, when he does make his escape, we do identify and sympathize with him, and with him taste freedom. He becomes the personification of it and for a moment we are even willing to overlook the fratricide he committed. But the escape is too easy, too sensational. It is not altogether convincing. It has something melodramatic about it. And for this reason we can hardly say that it is a *great* novel.

Such sensationalism as we find in *Falconer*, however, is as nothing compared to the sensationalism in Ian Fleming's novels, and in a host of spy, western, mystery and science-fiction stories. Only when a real attempt is made by the writer to be plausible and convincing can his work be considered serious fiction.

The strongest novels, I think, aren't necessarily those that have an elaborate plot but those that give the strongest impression of life.

Life is full of coincidences, but the use of coincidence in
fiction presents difficulties, because the writer is apt to use
coincidence as a tool to solve certain situations or to complicate them, tending to make the work seem contrived. In
life, of course, coincidences happen quite spontaneously;
they are not deliberate—nothing is less deliberate than
chance—and though they, too, may solve or complicate a
situation, they are not used as a tool. Coincidence, when
used in fiction, should give the impression of happening by
chance, quite naturally, and not artificially as a means to an
end that the writer has resorted to. Or, even more validly,
a story can be a study of coincidence, of chance, of accident, as in Thornton Wilder's *The Bridge of San Luis Rey* and
Vladimir Nabokov's reminiscences, *Speak Memory*, in which
he claims that the following of coincidences should be "the
true purpose of autobiography." Nabokov tells us of a Russian general who, when a guest at his home in St. Petersburg, opened a box of matches, set them in a straight line,
and said that it was the sea when calm. Then he set them in
a zigzag pattern, and said that it was the sea when rough. At
that moment the general was called away by a messenger to
go and take command of the collapsing Russian front in the
war against Japan in the Far East. Many years later, in
1918, during the revolution, the Nabokovs were walking
west toward Poland when someone coming up from behind
asked Nabokov's father for a match. It was that same general.

Many great writers—including Dickens, Victor Hugo,
F. Scott Fitzgerald and Thomas Hardy—have been ac-
cused of using too many coincidences and of overplotting.
But these writers abundantly make up for these flaws with

their splendid characterizations, or their ideas, or their poetry, or their humor.

A short story or a novel, like anything living, should grow and develop as it proceeds. As in life, there may be a sudden, unexpected turn in the events or course of the story. This may be called a twist. Often ironic, a twist usually runs counter to what preceded it. It frequently has something oblique and subtle about it. A story always needs form, longs for form, and if a twist is rooted in causality, that is, if there is strong reason for it in the story, if it is well founded, if it is an integral part of the natural, spontaneous form of the narrative, then it is welcome, then it can enrich and even make the story. But if it is an artificial distortion in the plot, a blob that comes out of the blue without cause, then it is no better than a *deus ex machina*—a last-minute device contrived to undo the entanglement that the author has got himself into. The *deus ex machina* was originally a god suddenly lowered onto the stage to decide the outcome of a play. Because it resembles a *deus ex machina*, the introduction of an important character toward the end of a novel or story is best avoided. John Fowles says that "it is a time-honored rule" not to do so, though I don't believe there are any unbreakable rules in fiction. To cite an example of my no-rules thesis: I am writing about a girl who has a serious case of tuberculosis. The time is 1945. Everyone expects her to die. But the unexpected discovery of streptomycin, like the *deus ex machina* of long ago, determines the outcome: the girl is cured.

No discussion of plot is complete without some reference to beginnings and endings. And since we have just dealt with twists, let us consider tricky or surprise endings, though it isn't easy to find examples of trick twists and endings in serious contemporary fiction, for they have become most unfashionable. O. Henry, Maupassant, and even Chekhov (see his short story "The Bet") used them. I think it is true to say that the more the story needed them, the better they worked. A tricky ending may be no more than an exercise in deception, and the same may be said of a surprise ending, unless that surprise has some causal relationship with what came before, a strong link with it, some reason that stems from the story itself. Then, and especially if it comes as a revelation, shedding light on the rest of the story, a surprise ending is valid. As for surprises, one could say that anything original comes as a surprise to whoever finds it. In this sense, "surprise" has a beautiful meaning. Indeed, any original idea, image, felicitous rhyme or turn of phrase comes as a surprise, a gift to writer and reader alike.

I wrote a story entitled "The Emergency"* about an inexperienced army doctor in the Italian Alps. The post, he is told, may seem easy to him until something goes wrong. For months all is routine, then an emergency comes for which the young doctor is totally unprepared. Two men are carried in in a state that would seem to tax the skill of even the best of surgeons. As the doctor makes ready to treat them, his hands tremble, his mind is flustered. And then he realizes, or rather he is told, that the two men are dead. He is shamefully relieved. Now, in this story the ending comes as a surprise to protagonist and reader alike, but the surprise is rooted in the story. The whole story

---

* *The New Yorker* (March 4, 1972).

foreshadows some kind of an emergency. The story leads up to it and depends on it, just as the ending depends on what led up to it. It isn't just a trick, a device—and in no small part because truth was the guide.

A short story I wrote entitled "The Change"* deals with a man who in 1978, looking back on his past, realizes that each year ending with an eight has brought a change in his life. He lives in a studio near the house in which his wife lives; they have drifted apart over the years. He waits for a change to take place and has the feeling that every woman he meets will effect it, but nothing happens until, on New Year's Eve, just before midnight, in the depth of his sadness and loneliness, his wife knocks at his studio door, bringing a bottle of champagne and two glasses. The ending, I think now, comes too much as a surprise. I should probably have prepared the ground for the reunion, made it more logical.

Often the end and the beginning of a story have a certain similarity; the ending evokes the beginning or is an echo of it. If skillfully done and if the story calls for it, such an ending will bring the story full circle, as in Bernard Malamud's "Black Is My Favorite Color." If unskillfully done, on the other hand, such an ending may seem too pat, too easy, too contrived or deliberate.

As for beginnings, I think one ought to try to write first sentences and opening paragraphs that reach as close to the middle of the story as one dares. To begin, as nature does, without preface. To get right into the core of the story. To set the tone of the whole thing in the opening scene. The

---

* *TriQuarterly 46* (Fall 1979).

reader is thus intrigued from the start and reads on. Ideally one sentence should lead up to the next till the end of the book. If one does have this sort of an opening, sooner or later, all sorts of questions will be raised in the mind of the reader; the author himself will feel that he has ventured too far. At this point he will have to supply information, background material, answer the questions that the reader silently poses. This the writer may do through flashbacks, retrospective writing.

A flashback—a term that like "close-up" (close-range, intimate visualization) comes to us from motion pictures—means retrospective writing. An example:

> He wished that long, long ago he had taken a step he hadn't taken—a jump, really.
>
> It was in July, 1940, and he was on the Ettrick, a Polish liner taken over by the English when the Nazis invaded Poland. The ship was loaded with German prisoners of war—most of them airmen—and interned civilians. . . .
>
> Sitting in the armchair, he wished he had jumped and reached the riverbank. . .*

When not done deftly, a flashback can be a tedious interruption in the narrative. But it isn't enough to handle a flashback deftly: it must be as interesting as the rest of the story or chapter; it must have immediacy. Though the flashback takes place in the past, it should seem to live now, and like the present, should have the urgency, the mystery, of the future in it. Usually, at the beginning of a flashback, the past perfect tense is used, but very soon the

---

*"The Jump" (*The New Yorker*, January 6, 1973).

writer should shift to the past tense and keep to it until he shifts back to the past perfect to indicate the end of the flashback. To keep the past perfect throughout, with all its "had's" and "had been's," would make the flow of narrative too heavy. A flashback is often followed by the word "now," as the story returns to the present. A double space is useful to denote such a time shift and also to indicate an important lapse of time, change of setting, or new action. A flashback in a story in the present tense is written without the use of the past perfect. This is, in fact, one of the advantages of present-tense narrative, which fiction writers use to make the story more vivid, more immediate, more direct. In using flashbacks the writer must always remember that too much background information will weigh on the story, will tend to make the narrative heavy. Whatever a story is, it isn't a mass of information. And certainly there are no rules for fiction. That is its beauty. In writing a character sketch or a story about a place, perhaps a lengthy description of the person or place at the beginning is warranted. I am only trying to say what has worked in my experience. Everyone should follow his own fancy, his inclination, and write in the way that comes most naturally to him, taking nothing for granted.

The middle of a novel—it has been said—should be broad. Yet one often reads fine linear, episodic stories and novels, for example, Salinger's novel *The Catcher in the Rye*.

To go back to endings, Max Beerbohm once said that there is no happy or sad ending, and that there is only the inevitable ending—in life and in fiction. The inevitable ending: the ending that makes all the other endings look wrong, the ending beside which all other endings are more or less false.

I don't know whether one can say that the reader of
today, though he has more books to choose from, is less
gullible and more sophisticated than the reader of a century
ago. What is certain is that no less than the reader of the
past, he is always looking for something new. The best
writer follows no dotted line. If one draws one's plots from
one's observations and experience, the danger of retracing
worn paths—and one must blaze new ones, cover new
ground, explore—is greatly reduced, for life renews itself
continuously, not only with each generation, but with each
individual. Isaac Bashevis Singer's stories, for example,
have the ring of truth and often a distinct biographical or
autobiographical flavor. His short story "Safe Deposit"* is
about an old man (and Singer is not young, except at
heart) who goes from Florida to New York where he has a
safe deposit box in a bank. He gets hopelessly lost in what
once was his city and is in danger of losing not only his
savings, but his life. A woman befriends him, takes him to
her house, warms him, restores him. The story ends on a
happy note (rare in realistic fiction), but the happy ending
here, given the characterizations, is the inevitable ending,
and therefore quite convincing.

If a writer makes an outline for a novel and if, as the
novel progresses, it tends to diverge from the outline, I
think the writer should let it diverge. To make the novel
follow that outline too strictly will stiffen and cramp it. Like
a plant, it should be allowed freedom. The outline should
be altered, not the novel.

---

* *The New Yorker* (April 13, 1979).

When one comes to the climax and the dénouement of the story, the ending should come soon and swiftly. It's no use dribbling on and on—the interest has waned.

Because so much in life has no conclusion, writers, especially in this century, have given their stories or novels an open ending. Some of Michelangelo's statues have an artfully unfinished look that lends them an infinite quality, something more essential, more whole, more complete than any finish, completion or ending can give. And this, I suppose, is the author's goal or hope in the open ending.

Just as form cannot be separated from content, so plot cannot be separated from the writing itself. To describe the plot of a beautiful book in other than the author's own words is to diminish it to the limit of recognition. I like to think of plot not as a stiff, rigid, fixed frame, plan, pattern, scheme or skeleton on which one builds a story, but as something growing with the writing, inextricable from it and undergoing the same changes, turning the same corners, never entirely preconceived. To experiment means to try and to see what comes out; one does not know until the experiment is over. Any story or novel should be viewed as an experiment.

6

THEME

T HE theme is the underlying concept of a story. I wrote
a short story entitled "The Cane."* The subject is
beating in an English boarding school, but the theme is the
indignity of corporal punishment. Again, the subject of a
story of mine called "Beppa"** is a weekend trip that a
streetwalker and a medical sublieutenant take together, but
the theme is a woman's dignity.

Life's most significant themes are freedom, love, and
death. And I think it is of some value to try to relate any
theme to these three great forces. Thus the indignity of
corporal punishment might be related to freedom, or to the
infringement of personal freedom, or to love, or to want of
love. And so might the theme of dignity. Power, money,
authority, careers, work, and education have something to
do with independence, and therefore with freedom. Dedi-

---

* *The New Yorker* (April 18, 1959).
** *Antaeus* 34 (Summer 1979).

cation to one's work—to medical research, for example, as in Sinclair Lewis's *Arrowsmith*—has to do with knowledge, and with love of humankind. Birth, too, could be related to love, for man is born of love; with birth new love arises, and each loving encounter is a rebirth. Loneliness, disillusionment, difficulty in connecting, could be related to love or the lack of it.

The great appeal that stories about escape from prison have might be explained by the sympathy that whoever seeks freedom receives: for a moment, if we can forget his crime, the person escaping becomes the embodiment of freedom, freedom's flag flying. I have written a short story entitled "The Jump,"* about a step that if taken might have led to freedom. The step wasn't taken, but failure can be more cognitive than success. The person who is deprived of freedom, or of love, may know it more deeply than the one who is enjoying it. Freedom is related to one's conscience, and stories about guilt, remorse, and alienation are also about freedom. Mysteries and detective stories attract so many readers not just because of the puzzle they pose, but because of death—its mystery, its awesomeness, its finality. If the victims were merely to be wounded the story would lose much of its force.

Theoretically one should be able to write a good story or a novel even about some relatively insignificant matter— the loss of a purse, for instance. In losing a purse, a person goes through some anguish or anxiety or annoyance. She may spend hours looking for it without being in the least bored. And if she finds it, there may be a moment of joy, a

* *The New Yorker* (January 6, 1973).

climax, and a dénouement. A writer might be able to make
these experiences live as vividly in his story as they do in
real life, but it would be difficult to do so. The writer
would, in other words, be handicapped by the slightness of
the event. To make such a story significant one would
probably have to make the person very poor indeed. The
story then would acquire meaningfulness—the recovery of
the purse would mean freedom from want. Freedom would
again be the theme. It is a fact, I think, that the most common reason editors give for rejecting a story (if the story is
good enough to evoke a comment other than a rejection
slip) is that the story is "too slight," i.e., too much like an
anecdote, not significant enough. One can, indeed, write
about something slight and succeed—when the story is
humorous. But then, one is tempted to say that humor is
the theme.

Without a doubt, love is fiction's—and life's—most
important theme. But it isn't often that we read stories of
glowing passion, stories about the love for which one
laughs and cries in the manner of Tristan and Iseult. We
are more apt to read about infidelity, separation, im-
potence, jealousy, hate, possession—than about love. It is
as if the negative side of love were closer at hand, more
within reach, and as if the writer had to rely on the lack of
love to let the reader know what love is. It isn't easy to
write about real love without falling into the mawkish. But
it can be done, of course, and Brian Moore's *The Lonely
Passion of Judith Hearne* is an example.

Love has infinite aspects and variations. One has only to
think of love for one's children, one's parents, and of love
for animals, as in Marjorie Kinnan Rawling's novel *The*

Yearling; of lonely love as in Nathanael West's *Miss Lonely-hearts*, of love between people with some abnormality, as in Marjorie Kellogg's novel, *Tell Me That You Love Me, Junie Moon*, and to some extent in Carson McCullers's "The Ballad of the Sad Café," in which the heroine is in love with a dwarf.

At its best, erotic, sensual writing is closely linked to love as a theme. Some may even say that it's central. And certainly the most important recent development in fiction has been its emancipation from all moralistic fetters. No longer are there unprintable words or sexual scenes that a writer may not describe in graphic detail. The gory has always been permitted; why not the pornographic? But whether this new freedom has made the writing more erotic is open to question. The truly erotic is elusive.

Pornography, according to United States Supreme Court Justice Brennan, has not been adequately defined, and I won't try to do so here. Art and imagination go hand in hand, and will just as readily enter the pornographic as the sublime, the profane as the sacred. Often the writer feels compelled to use vulgar words in an effort to be realistic, and if it suits the characters or setting, he is justified. For why should only the genteel be faithfully portrayed? Pornography is widespread because, when well written, it reveals an important aspect of life, and people hope to feel more alive reading it. What is needed is to lend beauty to the pornographic. Only then will it be erotic. But frequently the spiritual side of love is ignored as constantly as the physical side of it was by some nineteenth-century writers. All too often pornography is cold and clinical, and even worse, mechanical. Pornography will be self-defeating, lifeless, when the

description could as well be applied to machines as to people.
I have read in a novel a passage describing or trying to reproduce the sounds made in a love scene. The intent was
erotic. Alas, it suggested nothing so much as the noises made
by an overloaded washing machine.

D.H. Lawrence's *Lady Chatterley's Lover* is erotic. The
author's purpose is to exalt and vindicate the beauty of
sensual experience, especially its highest moment:

> But it [that moment] came with a strange, slow thrust of
> peace, and ponderous, primordial tenderness, such as made
> the world at the beginning.

Such a moment is also well described by Joyce Carol Oates
in her novel *Do With Me What You Will:*

> With her lover everything was extinguished except his love:
> His demand for her . . . He loved her so much, needed her so
> violently, that she seemed almost to be extinguished in her
> own body and to enter her body again through his. Then she
> would feel that flash of pure, selfless triumph, the joy of her
> completion . . .

In my short story "Osage Orange,"* I have tried to
write about the wholeness and the eternal quality of such a
moment:

> In the extreme moment of passion she gave a cry that
> seemed to him to fill not just the room and house but the
> whole town, and to go out like a wave against the waves of the
> sea that bathed that town and to the sky. It echoed, that cry of
> joy, through the months that passed; it seemed to reach into

---

* *The New Yorker* (October 24, 1977).

eternity, even as it had reached into the universe. It would not die. . .

The erotic cannot be forced. A ribald entertainer may strive to be erotic, and, despite his pornographic vocabulary, fail miserably. On the other hand, a minister or a judge, denouncing a lusty, wanton woman, may, despite their intentions and refined language, paint an erotic picture of her. Henry James in *What Maisie Knew* and Nathaniel Hawthorne in his portrait of Hester Prynne at times achieve the erotic, puritanical writers though they may be. Similarly, the Bible (Proverbs 7) draws a very enticing picture of a woman, even as she is denounced and condemned.

A passage won't be erotic if at least one of the characters isn't attractive. John Updike's short story "Transaction"* is about a man who picks up a streetwalker and takes her to his hotel room. Most of the story takes place in bed, and it goes into detail about what they do there. But at the beginning of the story he introduces the girl by describing her as "far from pretty—bony, her narrow face school-teacherishly beaked." This unattractive picture of her, and the lack of passion and even warmth in the lovemaking, certainly don't help make the story erotic. It does have a point, since the characters are convincingly presented and the vocabulary is rich, but not an erotic point. Hence the love theme suffers. Judith Rossner, in her novel *Looking for Mr. Goodbar*, does bring a certain passion into her scenes and does achieve an erotic effect, but it is a passion flecked with more lust than love. It is a crude, raw kind of passion.

---

* First published in *Oui* magazine, and included in his short story collection *Problems and Other Stories* (Knopf).

Her love and tenderness she reserves for her pages about children. Philip Roth in *Portnoy's Complaint* has love scenes that are more funny than erotic. Henry Miller's fiction often does have the strong beat and erotic flavor of passion, and so do some of Jayne Anne Phillips's short stories.

In writing about the erotic aspect of the love theme, it should be remembered that the prospect, anticipation and expectation of love may be more stirring than love's fulfillment. I remember, for instance, reading with excitement about the hero of Stendhal's *The Red and the Black* climbing to the window of his mistress's bedroom. A picture in *Vogue* may be more suggestive than one in the centerfold of *Playboy*. The undetailed simplicity of a Modigliani nude may be more erotic than a photograph revealing every physical detail. The latter may spark curiosity more than desire. It is quite the same in writing—a few simple strokes may stir the reader's imagination more than an elaborate description. And, as in any other theme, it is essential that the story unfold artistically, convincingly, unpredictably. The more intense the love and the further away it is from the purely physiological, the more effective will the story be.

Death and what leads to it—illness, accident, war, murder, suicide—are everlasting themes, and death is prominent in many of the best-known novels of the past two generations—F. Scott Fitzgerald's *The Great Gatsby,* Theodore Dreiser's *An American Tragedy,* William Faulkner's *As I Lay Dying*, Ernest Hemingway's *For Whom the Bell Tolls,* Norman Mailer's *The Naked and the Dead,* William Styron's *Lie Down in Darkness*—to name but a few by American writers. Death is the substance of tragedy. The story can be told by those left behind, as by the son whose father dies in James Agee's *Death in the Family*. It can be a view of the holocaust as in André Schwartz-Bart's novel *The Last of the Just*. It can also be the death of hope, as in Sylvia Plath's *The Bell Jar*. It can be the story of a daughter's devotion to her father as in Mary Gordon's *Final Payments*, in which the narrator tells how she, alone and in the bloom of her life, took care of her paralyzed father for eleven years:

> You may wonder, as many have wondered, why I did it, why I stayed with my father all those years. Does it suggest both the monstrosity and the confusion of the issue if I say that the day Dr. MacCauley told me about my father's stroke was of my whole life the day I felt most purely alive? Certainty was mine, and purity; I was encased in meaning like crystal.

It is always the intensity with which things—death, illness, in this case—are felt that make what is written about them great or small. A novel—like Faulkner's *As I Lay Dying*—may indeed only tell of a funeral journey, but the suffering in each labored step of that journey suggests how meaningful the dead person was to the living.

Often the death theme and the love theme are linked, one complementing the other—the one really poignant moment in Erich Segal's *Love Story* occurs when Jenny is in her deathbed. To be truly tragic a novel must show the chasm that death is, the void that it leaves. The effect of someone's death on those left behind, and on the reader, depends on how much that person meant to them.

It isn't from a desire to write about death or from vague ideas about it, that short stories and novels with death as a theme stem, but rather from precise observations. I, for instance, have written several stories about people dying.

In "The Little Ark,"* the idea for it came from the protagonist's urge to furnish a summer house to which she
knew she would never return. She kept ordering things for
it by telephone, and she seemed to be outfitting a ship for
her long journey toward oblivion. In another story—"Last
Rites"**—about a woman artist who was never baptized,
never went to church, and who, for these reasons, was not
blessed by the priest as her casket was lowered into the
ground, the idea came to me from seeing the movement
that a mason made later as he flicked some mortar off his
trowel while covering the vault with terra-cotta tiles:

> That quick flicking of the trowel seemed to her son a kind of
> benediction, and the mortar that was flung from it holy water.
> She had never been fond of prayers, ceremonies, sermons; she
> had always been fond of watching skilled artisans at work. And
> this flipping of the trowel seemed so much more fitting, so
> much more to her taste, than any kind of religious benedic-
> tion. It seemed to lend a touch of joy and freshness to the
> burial . . . It was, after so much dreariness, a pleasant obser-
> vation; at last, it seemed to him, she had taken things in hand,
> in her own strong hands, and he could almost see them, those
> admirable hands, come alive again, directing, doing.

In yet another story of mine about death, "The Bell,"***
about an old man dying and ringing for his son, it was the
bell itself, its insistent ringing and the son's answering
those calls, that suggested the idea. The story deals partly
with euthanasia and with the son's thoughts about it after

---

* *The New Yorker* (November 19, 1966).
** *The New Yorker* (May 22, 1965).
*** *The New Yorker* (February 10, 1963).

Soft Core," "The Bell," "A Gallery of Women"*—two of
which are in the first person, three in the third. Since they
have two of the main characters in common and since the
theme is more or less the same in each one, I think I could
treat them as chapters of a novel, rewriting them all in
either the first or third person, without detracting from
their quality.

The first-person narrative is the more familiar of the two
forms in the sense that it is usually the one used in conversation, letters, diaries, and essays.

Whether a writer is aware of it or not, he also uses the
first person in an effort to be more convincing, to make the
story more real. It may add a measure of credibility to the
story. A reader is more likely to believe that something
took place when someone says, "I was there and saw it
happen," than when someone says, "He was there and saw
it happen." The former is a firsthand account, the latter is
secondhand. Of course, the credibility of a piece of fiction
is going to depend on many other factors besides the choice
of first- or third-person narrative. It will depend on the
beauty and the force of the writing itself, on the story, and
not on who is made to tell it. Yet, other things being
equal—and they hardly ever are—the first person may, as
I said, contribute to the believability of the narrative. And
if the narrative is more believable, it will also be more
vivid, more alive. It will sound true even if it never took
place. Conversely, though the event may have actually hap-

---

* *The New Yorker* (December 30, 1974; March 7, 1977; June 15, 1972; February
10, 1972; November 13, 1978).

pened in real life, if it is unconvincingly presented, then for our purposes, it is not true. Liveliness, directness, immediacy, truth, again don't depend on choice of point of view; but in choosing to use the first person one may, subconsciously or not, have these things in mind, and then the story may benefit from it.

In writing a first-person story without proper names— one in which the characters are designated by pronouns (I, he, she)—there will rarely be any doubt as to who is saying, thinking, feeling, or doing what. Using the third-person viewpoint, if the writer says, "He thought he would go away," the first "he" may refer to one person, the second to another, or both may refer to the same person. If, on the other hand, one writes, "I thought he would go away," there is no confusion. And it is often tedious and heavy to have to name the characters too frequently. Using the I of first-person viewpoint will obviate this. Thus, the first-person may add to the clearness and smoothness of the narrative.

The first-person viewpoint should probably not be used if the narrator is too much the hero of the story—someone, that is, upon whom great merit or praise is heaped. It is harder to be the "I hero" than the "I villain," or rogue. In other words, it is difficult to make oneself the great hero of a story.

I wrote a short story entitled "The Children,"* in which "I," the narrator, am driving across a very poor section of southern Italy with a friend. In a mountain village, a bunch of hungry-looking children crowd around us as we

---

* *The New Yorker* (March 10, 1975).

come out of a grocery store with a large bag of food and return to our open car. My friend, afraid of them, insists we leave in a hurry, and we do. The hasty departure spoils the trip for me, and later I must return to the village alone to give some food to those children. In this story, the narrator was too much the hero of it, so I reversed the roles. My friend became the hero, and I, the narrator, the one who insisted that we leave in a hurry.

Confessional stories—stories in which personal secrets are revealed—are usually in the first person. Occasionally, however, the secrets are such that the author is embarrassed to use the first person, even when—as is often the case—he uses a fictitious name for himself. In that situation, the writer should by all means use third person, for embarrassment might inhibit him and spoil the story. A story of mine, "The Change,"* deals with a married man who encounters several women one after another, as in a dance. The use of the first person in this story would have made me feel self-conscious, so I used the third.

The third person should also be used in stories in which the protagonist-narrator's life is endangered. If the first person is used in such a story, the reader will know that the protagonist-narrator lived to tell the tale, and much of the suspense will be lost as a result.

At present, I am in the process of writing a story about a boy who gets lost in the Canadian woods in a national park 100 miles north of Montreal. He remembers seeing in a school atlas a railroad line crossing Canada and running from the city of Quebec to Lake Superior. Knowing that

---

* *TriQuarterly 46* (Fall 1979).

sooner or later he will come to it, he walks due north following the Dipper at night, and mosses and lichens on trees in the daytime. In this story, I use the third person to increase the suspense, for the first person would be telltale, would provide the clue to a happy outcome—my survival!

Narration in the third person is more frequently used in fiction than first-person narration, probably because the third-person viewpoint lends the writer a greater sense of perspective, a certain distance from which he may view things more effectively, a wider horizon, a greater range. This state of being detached or removed, of being able to see things from a distance or through a keyhole, may work to the writer's advantage.

A novel written from a single point of view—be it first or third person—precludes omniscience. The narrator won't be able to enter into the minds of the other characters, i.e. he won't be able to know for sure what they are thinking or feeling, or even what they are doing, if he is not present. And this may be a serious limitation. On the other hand, he may be able to work quite comfortably within this narrow, but perhaps more concentrated, more focused world, and then the single point of view may be used to no disadvantage whatever. It will, in fact, lend unity to the novel.

One way a fiction writer can overcome some of the limitations imposed by narrative from a single point of view is to use words such as: visibly, evidently, obviously, clearly, presumably, apparently, conceivably, as if, as though, assume, seem, look, appear, suppose, and the like.

Here are some examples: "I assumed he was going to leave." "They had evidently arranged to meet at the house." "She was visibly affected." "She had obviously not forgiven him." "She sat down as though she were already feeling giddy."

The narrator may or may not be the protagonist. He may, in fact, be a fairly minor character, but he is always an important observer. I wrote a short story entitled "The Orchard,"* about a man with three sons. He plants an orchard that will take care of his daily needs in his old age. The story is written from the point of view of one of the sons, a relatively unimportant character in it, but a careful observer.

Sometimes, as in the novels of Joseph Conrad, the narrator introduces a character, and then this character tells the story in the first person. It is an attempt to make the story more authentic, but this device—a story within a story—has lost favor among most contemporary novelists.

In a novel written from an omniscient point of view—a rather presumptuous term; *multiple* or *shifting* point of view may be more accurate—the author describes places and times and portrays the various characters. He knows and relates what they are thinking, feeling, saying, doing, wherever they are.

The point of view will continually shift. The reader may wonder how the author knows so much. A single point of view may be considered more plausible, and, indeed, Joan Didion writes: "We are uneasy about a story until we know who is telling it." But if the novel is convincing, such questions won't arise in the reader's mind—he will be

---

* *The New Yorker* (June 15, 1968).

swept by the narrative, following each character's thoughts, feelings and actions.

Sometimes, as in Faulkner's *As I Lay Dying*, an event will be told as seen from the point of view of the several characters involved, in succession. The event will be the same and yet will not be the same because it will differ according to who is telling it. The impression of the event upon the character is given relevance, and the way he recounts it characterizes him—as his view of it colors the occurrence.

The omniscient or multiple point of view allows great freedom, has almost no limitations. A novel written in multiple viewpoint may, on the other hand, be less unified, more rambling, more disconnected, and less believable, than a novel written from one point of view. Unity, of course, won't depend on technicalities; yet even such a technical device as viewpoint may help unify the novel, especially when felt by the author as a necessity, inherent to the novel, something that he can't do without, something that if not used would not just alter but distort the very spirit of his work.

All sorts of techniques are used in writing fiction, and sometimes an author will write a section in the first person, another in the third (as in J.D. Salinger's short story "For Esmé—With Love and Squalor"), and the single and multiple points of view will be used in different parts of a novel. A method, rarely used today, is the epistolary, in which the novel, or a large part of it, is written in the form of a series of letters. A good example of this is George Moore's *The Lake*. At times, as in Ivy Compton-Burnett's writing, the novels consist almost entirely of dialogue. Variations in point of view are far more common in the novel than in the short story. Short stories, especially nowadays, are most often written from a single point of view. But there are certainly many examples of great short stories in which the point of view shifts, as in D.H. Lawrence's story, "The Horse Dealer's Daughter." A shift in point of view in a short story can be disruptive, but in the hands of a good writer, the shift can be so smooth as to be almost unnoticeable and absolutely unobtrusive. As the story becomes dramatic and reaches its climax, the point of view from which it is written is lost sight of more and more; it becomes secondary, fades into the background; the characters assume a life of their own.

Whatever the point of view, the author in modern fiction has his characters present his views, keeps in the background, and doesn't enter into the reader's confidence or throw asides to him.

The writer who is undecided as to whether he is going to write his story in first or third person, or from the single or multiple viewpoint, will have to weigh all these factors. Very often, however, the choice of viewpoint comes naturally, and in those instances, the natural choice is likely to be the best. The wise writer will choose the viewpoint with which he feels most comfortable for the particular story he is going to write—the one that will impose the fewest limitations, will most effectively embrace and carry the whole story, will help him tell it with the greatest impact.

8

HUMOR IN FICTION

THROUGH humor even a slight, trivial incident can become the valid subject of a story. Take the case, for example, of an awkward young man who, on a hot day, is invited to lunch, asked by the host to take his coat off, and then to put it on again, because he is wearing suspenders. Such an incident is much too slight for a short story, but if it were written with humor, as it is not here, then it could pass as a valid story. Humor has this wonderful power: it can give uniqueness to the ordinary, lightness to the heavy, sheen to the dull. By humorous treatment, the event, no matter how slight, can become worth recounting.

The light touch is rare and few are the writers who possess it. Humor, in fiction, usually comes to the fore in dialogue. F. Scott Fitzgerald in *The Great Gatsby* is at his funniest when Gatsby speaks and uses the expression "old sport," which he does very often but always unexpectedly.

But of course, humor, wayward spirit that it is, won't be confined to dialogue, won't be confined period. Even plain narrative in the hands of P.G. Wodehouse can be funny. His slapstick is served with white gloves, and he knows so intimately his butlers and the foibles and idiosyncrasies of the people they work for.

Woody Allen in his stories comments and plays on many of the mores and misconceptions of the day, and at the same time creates characters who shift in a moment from the passionate to the pathetic, from the matter-of-fact to the poetic.

In Joseph Heller's *Catch-22*, the humor lies in sarcasm, irony, and satire, as deals are made and the ulterior motives and incompetence of those who are in a position of authority play havoc with the lives of those who are not.

To be effective, humorous fiction depends on originality, spontaneity, and on seeing things in a curious, droll way. It has a spirit that defies definition or explanation. It is leaven, it is life. It is elusive: it calls for naturalness and resents obvious efforts to seek it out, i.e., a writer usually is not funny if he tries to be, if the effort shows. Good, humorous stories need a certain casualness. The very same words told by one character might be funny, by another fall flat. The way in which the joke is told becomes the substance of it. The atmosphere, the right moment, the situation, the setting, the ambiance, the audience itself, and the mood of the audience are also important in creating a humorous effect. And suggestion—not stating everything, leaving the obvious out, letting the reader bridge the gap— plays a role. Humor resents a preface or an introduction: if a character says, "The funniest thing happened," then the reader (or other characters in the story) will expect too much and will inevitably be disappointed.

Imitation, mimicry, mockery are often funny; so are the outrageous, the preposterous (as in J.P. Donleavy's *The Ginger Man* and Gore Vidal's *Myra Breckenridge*, in which the humor borders on the cruel, and a reader is almost ashamed of laughing), the zany, the odd, the naive, the candid (as in A.A. Milne's *Winnie the Pooh*), the incongruous, the unexpected, the risqué. Frequently, as in parodies and satire, the humor is loaded with comment and criticism. S.J. Perelman cavorts and frolics with language, expressions, and peculiar facts. Wit, double meanings, puns, understatement, exaggeration, irony, and even sarcasm (as in Ring Lardner's "The Golden Honeymoon") can be funny, but again, as with other forms of art, they have to be original, new, spirited. In fact, in Italian the word for humorous is *spiritoso*. Accent, cadence, inflection, use of local expressions, regionalisms, dialect, help.

Sometimes, all too rarely, there is a touch of poetry in humorous fiction—as in Mark Twain's *Huckleberry Finn* and *The Adventures of Tom Sawyer*.

Funny lines often aren't funny when taken out of the context of the story or novel. They need the tension of the context in order to be lively.

9

FORM AND STYLE

WHETHER one is writing a poem or a story, or doing a painting, the form it will take is the challenge—and the wonder—of it. When writers talk about a story not jelling, crystallizing, binding, about its not being completely distilled, leavened, fermented, transfigured, they are saying that it lacks form. They mean that it is still an uncoordinated mass of words, a pile of information, heavy and raw, put together rather than created. In other words, it has no life. It is still inert matter. Form is matter transcended.

In architecture, a building has form when the enormous weight of steel and glass and concrete assumes spiritual lightness. In painting, form is achieved when inert pigment becomes active color; in dancing, when the body becomes pure expression. In writing and composing, the process is less obvious, for words and notes are not as solid as steel, glass, concrete, pigment and the body, but they can be just as heavy, and just as readily can they be turned into essence.

Closely linked to form is unity. Without unity there is no form and there is no life. Anything living—and a short story or any work of art can be viewed as "living"— resents and resists being divided. It clings to every part of itself. Unity isn't primarily a question of place, time, action, uniformity of tone or of tense or of point of view. All of these things, as well as rhyme, refrain, artful repetition, simplicity of plot, a recurring phrase, coming full circle or a certain similarity or echo between the beginning and the end, symmetry, continuity, juxtaposition, the title, will tend to lend unity to a story, but they don't constitute unity. Unity is more subtle and more elusive. A story can have all these ingredients and still miss unity, still miss coming alive. Unity is life, it is the soul of a story. It is an idea taking hold and growing with and in every word, every sentence. It will astonish the author himself in the end. Because it exceeds his hopes, his expectations. Because the result is greater than the sum total of its parts. Because it is something new, in the fullest and richest meaning of the word—something not out of a mold, that does not follow a formula, but fresh, blessed with originality.

Sometimes the unity of a story will not be apparent till a certain line—and it may be the very last—is written. That line, that revelation, will bring the whole thing to life. Saul Bellow's novella *Seize the Day* is about a day in the life of Tommy Wilhelm, an impractical, weak and very human person. It has the unity of time (one day), place (New York City), action (his trying to cope with the stress and strain of life), point of view (it is told from his viewpoint); and the title itself with its encompassing quality lends it unity. But it would miss having form and real unity if it didn't also have essential unity. It has no slack, no dead weight. It is leavened; it has humor; and in the end, it makes a point: Tommy, wandering into a funeral chapel, is overwhelmed by a sense of brotherhood, communion. All men are his neighbors as he weeps uncontrollably over someone he does not even know.

Again, in Carson McCullers's novelette, "The Ballad of the Sad Café," about a woman who falls under the spell of a dwarf, there is that strong love and exultation of life. Life runs through every line, giving form to the story.

Art is giving one's ideas a form that will make them convincing. In the process of being expressed, the germinal idea will grow, will become more convincing. Thus form and idea can hardly be separated.

The idea is what tightens a story and gives it unity and form. In such a story, the idea will illumine each page; there will be no opaque sentences. The first glimmer of an idea is quite often expressed early in the story, sometimes in the very first sentence. A short story I wrote entitled "Star Lake"* begins: *Sometimes I wish things so intensely they happen.* The story is about a boy in a lonely research station in the Canadian woods, daydreaming about sleeping with the only girl up there—his boss's wife. The next three sentences go: *But the circumstances through which they come about, the ways chosen to let me have what I want, are invariably quite different from those I had in mind. It's as if fate cared only about the end, not the means. And often I feel responsible, even guilty in the end for the outcome.* The rest of the story, which

---

* *The New Yorker* (May 17, 1958).

tells what actually happened, illustrates that first paragraph. Those first lines guided me through the clutter of
details and the maze of happenings, leading me to only the
most essential. This opening paragraph set me on the right
course in the maze and gave me control. No detail, no
happening in the story was extraneous to that idea, to that
first paragraph.

Similarly, in my short story, "The Fall,"* about rock
climbing, the idea stemmed from my watching, in a documentary film, a zebra succumbing to a lion, and I began
the story: *When they have no more strength and they give up the
fight, does the swimmer love the sea in which he drowns, the climber
the mountainous height that will make fatal his fall, the zebra the
lion that devours it? When they are past fear, when fear is behind
them. I have watched, in a documentary film, a zebra succumbing,
and I believe I saw a moment of love as it yielded. And I have
fallen, rock climbing.* Again, the rest of the story is a telling
of the incident, illustrating, giving body to that idea.

But, of course, the idea doesn't have to be expressed at
the beginning. In fact, it may not be expressed explicitly at
all, and only be conveyed through the narrative, the
incident, the plot, the character study. In a short story I
wrote entitled "The Orchard,"** about a man putting all
of his savings into a peach orchard, caring for it against
great odds, the idea, the point—expressed three-quarters of
the way through the story—is this: *It was as if some future
need, hardly surmised or suspected, were directing the course of his
actions.* In his old age and toward the end of the story, it is

---

* *The New Yorker* (July 1, 1961).
** *The New Yorker* (June 15, 1968).

the peach orchard that supplies him with enough money for his everyday needs. That idea, though not stated at the beginning, guided me through the story and knit the story together, lending it unity and form. And not only that: it gave me the energy to write it.

In this connection let me say that writers depend on ideas for their energy. A strong idea will give you a great urge to write. Ideas are more felicitous fonts of energy than will power and discipline.

Sometimes form is used almost as a synonym for style. But form is a more comprehensive term than style. Form, unlike style and rhythm to a certain extent, cannot be parodied. One could parody Faulkner's prose style or Dylan Thomas's rhythm, but not their form.

That is not to say that style does not have an inward, profound meaning. A writer's style is that writer's self.

So understood—when it isn't just mannerism, fashion, or convention—style, too, can't be easily separated from content.

Style is the writer's particular way of saying things, his way of expressing himself. It is the imprint—unmistakable, always recognizable—that a writer leaves on the page. It is what distinguishes one writer from another. What he writes is the content; the way he writes it is the style. But since what he writes is affected by the way he writes it, content and style are one.

Texture, which is related to style, may be thought of as the grain, the fabric, the warp and the woof of writing, its essence, its substance. It results from the choice of the words and the way they are linked, the details of the story's minute structure rather than its overall framework—the connections between characters and incidents and the sequence of episodes or events.

Grammatical writing, desirable as it is, does not of itself constitute style. Indeed, ungrammatical writing could in some instances be said to have style, as in stream-of-consciousness writing, or when the story is written from the point of view of a semiliterate person. When mistakes are made deliberately, they should be put in skillfully, i.e., there shouldn't be any doubt that they are there for a purpose, lest the reader take them for misprints or actual errors by the writer himself.

The sentence, "The important thing for us to ask ourselves is whether we should go on existing or whether we should put an end to our existence," can easily be shortened and improved in many ways, but these would all fall short of Shakespeare's solution, "To be, or not to be: that is the question." The essential—and elusive—element in style is originality.

A personal, distinctive rhythm, an elegant turn of phrase, a felicitous expression, a detail accurately drawn, vivid dialogue, or a word that is absolutely right can bring a story to life. The opening sentence of Tennessee Williams's short story, "The Resemblance between a Violin Case and a Coffin," for example, has a subtle rhythm and cadence that is quite characteristic of his work:

> With her advantage of more than two years and the earlier maturity of girls, my sister moved before me into that country of mysterious differences where children grow up.

That sentence has a delicate tone that suits the intimate quality of the story: content and style go together.

Here is a passage from my short story, "The Rats."* It is about the moment of freedom that people experience when they are fired or resign from a job. The protagonist is a research worker who quits because he finds his work futile, useless, and cruel to the rats he has been experimenting on.

> As I left the Institute and went home, I felt very, well—lightfooted, buoyant, weightless. This always happens to me when I give something up: There are a few moments, before my thoughts turn to the things that will have to be done, during which I am only thinking of the things I won't have to be doing any longer.

The lines express lightheartedness, and the rhythm of the last sentence enhances the meaning.

Another example of "rhythm" and its importance in fiction writing is found in Virginia Woolf's short story, "A Haunted House":

> Stooping, holding their silver lamp above us, long they look and deeply. Long they pause. The wind drives straightly; the flame stoops slightly. Wild beams of moonlight cross both floor and wall, and, meeting, stain the faces bent; the faces pondering; the faces that search the sleepers and seek their hidden joy.

The rhythm shouldn't be too obvious, or the reader will tend to ask why the author didn't write a poem instead of a story. The following is from the climax of a short story of mine, "The Fall":

---

* *The New Yorker* (April 22, 1961).

I could hardly hold the grasp a moment longer, yet the moments passed and I held on still. My fingers were like claws on the rocky face. Behind me was open, airy space. I felt myself becoming weak and panting. As though I could hang on with my teeth I bit the rock. The would-be bite was but a parting kiss. Holding nothing, by nothing withheld, I rested for a moment in the abyss.

The rhythm here may be slightly too obvious. There are even two rhymes (face/space, kiss/abyss), but the editors raised no objections.

Alliteration—the repetition of consonant sounds in successive words—can also lend a poetic quality to prose, as in the sentence, "He longed for love to liven his life." Onomatopoeia—the use of words whose sounds suggest their meaning, as *buzz* and *hiss*—can also help achieve this effect.

In contrast to poetic style, there is the plain, simple, almost matter-of-fact, terse, spare style of Hemingway with his short, clipped sentences, as in this example from his short story, "The Three-Day Blow":

Nick said nothing.... Bill wasn't there.... He wasn't drunk.... It was all gone.... That was all that mattered. He might never see her again. Probably he never would. It was all gone, finished.

Conciseness is the cornerstone of style. Brevity is often elegant. If something can be said in a few words, why use more? Rereading a short story of mine, "The Lighthouse,"* I find that the following sentence has fifteen words too many: "I felt like an intruder, someone who was

---

* *The New Yorker* (January 20, 1968).

trying to take somebody else's place without having a right to it.'' The first part of the sentence is quite sufficient; the rest only defines intruder and is superfluous. Here is another example: "There aren't many towns near Rome, and what other towns there are can't be called cities; in fact they are quite small.'' The sentence is long, awkward, and uninteresting. The writer needs to shorten it, lighten it, make it more incisive, give it style. It could read, for example, "Rome has few neighbors and none of any size.''

There are no absolute rules in fiction, but writing as succinctly as possible is advisable, as long as a writer doesn't do it at the expense of clarity and sound unintentionally curt. If overwriting is a fault, so is overpunctuating. The excessive use of subclauses, parentheses, or dashes can interrupt the flow of the story and give it a hiccupping effect. Periods, too, can be overused. There is no point in having several short sentences when one sentence will serve the purpose as well. Breaking up a sentence into several short ones can make the writing look simplistic. Overparagraphing should also be avoided, especially in a novel. But there are exceptions—sometimes, as in music or in drama, there is a need for frequent pauses. Using the word "and" too often tends to make the writing monotonous. I have listened to people tell stories till I lost the thread of them, and all I could hear was the word "and" repeated. I don't mean to say that a series of "and's" can't be effectively used. In the Bible and in certain passages of modern stories and novels the use of "and" can emphasize continuation and development and even lend solemnity and drama to the story.

Long sentences do have their place—when every word
counts; when the lengthy sentences of dialogue are appropriate to the character speaking; when they sound natural
to the writer. We have only to look at Faulkner's work for
examples. His sentences are often like waves that waft the
reader along with them.

Elegance and grace of phrasing are important. "Strike a
light and you cast a hundred shadows"; "I have written
with a certain success about failure"; "They [his paintings]
revealed to him things that would have lain forever undisclosed." Such well-turned phrases or felicitous expressions as these, in which two words are contrasted or
balanced (*light* and *shadows, success* and *failure, revealed* and
undisclosed), show a certain love of language and thoughtful-
ness that are indications of good style.

Repetition, appropriately and purposefully used, can
also add to the effectiveness of style. But careless, needless
repetition, combined with errors in punctuation, word use,
and grammar, are what editors most commonly fault
manuscripts with. In this kind of repetition, the rarer the
word the less it will bear being repeated: for instance, one
can hardly use the unfamiliar word "nugatory" more than
once in a story, for it stays in the reader's mind, while
a word like "small" can be used several times without
having the reader notice the repetition. And, on the other
hand, there is repetition that may sometimes help unify a
story or a novel, binding one paragraph to the next:

. . . And I did many things I had never done before—flew
kites, went roller-skating, explored caves draped with stalac-
tites, paddled in the pools left by the tide, visited a lighthouse.

Visited a lighthouse. I climbed the spiral staircase and knocked on the door up at the top....*

The repetition may be an image—a coiled copperhead, as in Joan Didion's novel *Play It As It Lays*. Or it may be a musical phrase, or the taste of a cookie dipped in tea, as in Marcel Proust's *Remembrance of Things Past*. Such words or phrases recurring here and there like threads in the texture of the story may help unify and strengthen the whole. Repetition of a word or phrase in dialogue can effectively distinguish one character from another. Sometimes a writer will deliberately begin two chapters of a novel in the very same way in order to lead the reader back to a certain time or recall that time for him (cf. George Moore's novel *Esther Waters*).

Incisive, accurate, relevant detail makes a narrative more distinctive, convincing, atmospheric—qualities that all contribute to style. I recently read an unpublished story about two lovers meeting in a dark bar. The clutter of irrelevant details was cancelled by the darkness, and that in itself seemed to me skillful. There was visible only the flash of an eye, the gleam of a glass, the flame of a candle. The atmosphere for the tryst was just right from the start—intimate, secret.

Sometimes one hears the expression, "Written in loving detail." The word "loving" applied to detail is apt and meaningful, though not, of course, if it's taken to mean that the author is indulging in love for his own words. Detail has to be faithful and essential. It shouldn't be an inventory,

---

* "The Lighthouse," *ibid.*

which is fine for a landlord but not for a writer. The reader entrusts himself to the writer and wants to see a scene through the writer's eye. This can happen only when the writer identifies with the object. Only then will the reader see such an object as a reflection in the mind of the writer. As a writer perceives a scene or object and makes it his, he gives it his imprint, endows it with his style, his way of looking at it.

As an example of a detailed and "loving" description, I will quote the passage about lichens from a short story of mine, "Of Love and Friendship"*:

> Pale green and yellow, orange and gray, tenuous blue, silver and almost white, spread by the wind or growing by contiguity, they improved the looks of almost anything they stuck to. Nor did they interfere with the host, except to give it cover. They made the tile roofs golden. They grew on ugly walls and monuments until their ugliness quite faded. They contributed to ruins part of their weathered look. They were the hand of time, its patina, its gift, or an instrument it wielded. And if you looked at them closely you saw the marvel of their structure: lacework, filigree, touch-me-not golden curls. Always an adornment on the bare. How did nature manage to be so unerringly tasteful? Was it, as with the clouds, the magic hand of chance?

Again from a story I wrote,** here is a passage describing a character in detail:

> I see him—a tall, thin man in a glen-plaid, double-breasted suit, and a silk tie—walking down the street, alone, as usual. One is apt to meet him any time, but especially at this hour of

---

* "Of Love and Friendship" (*The New Yorker*, May 26, 1973).
** "The Prince" (*The New Yorker*, May 11, 1963).

the night, when Verona begins to look deserted. Holding himself a little stiffly, as though there were some danger of his falling, he walks an undulating course. One hand stretches a trouser pocket. The other holds a cigarette—for elegance's sake. And he smiles. The smile is his most distinguishing feature. It is constant, unperturbed, contented. He wears it like his tie. He is looking straight in front of him, yet he could be looking at the sky. He hasn't seen me yet. I swear he hasn't, though we are awfully close.

Originality of style in depicting details will make them stand out, and lend them more truth. Details will make the story more believable. If the overall story line is invented and is somewhat sensational and slightly unconvincing, then details that are drawn from the author's experience will add a measure of veracity to that narrative and make it more credible, give it validity. In describing something of which the author presumably has no direct experience—a bank robbery, for instance—he will instinctively write in detail about a bank he is familiar with, a teller he has seen. The details will be real and will make the robbery seem more true.

Irrelevant, ordinary, inaccurate detail will deaden the story, will weight it down like ballast. The writer must constantly resist the temptation to include a beautifully written passage that just doesn't belong.

In fiction we need to heed what rings true, and discard the rest. Now, exaggeration and understatement are, literally speaking, departures from reality, for they tend to alter the truth. Must we discard them? Not always; certainly not understatement. Exaggeration may be quite funny. In J.D. Salinger's *The Catcher in the Rye*, Holden Caulfield tells what a light sleeper his mother is: "... all you have to do to my mother is cough somewhere in Siberia and she'll hear you." And understatement may be very suggestive and lend credibility to what is said.

Saying something with restraint may heighten the effect. If, for example, in describing an accident one says, "It wasn't a pretty sight," it might be more effective than "It was a dreadful sight." And "I haven't been altogether inactive," may be more telling than "I have been working like mad." Or, again, "I know that every book will not please you" may be more incisive than, "I know that you are very critical." And in context, two lovers saying, "We didn't read anymore," will suggest a love scene.

At times a vivid picture may be presented by coupling an exaggeration with an understatement, as in the following sentence:

> Just as she tumbled through the door it seemed as if the world had come to an end above her; two barrels of a shotgun discharged into a room make a noise.*

A writer's awareness of a poorly written passage depends on his taste and his ability to judge his work objectively. Sometimes when I am in doubt about a sentence I have written, I read it aloud to myself twice—the first time as well as I can, and the second time as badly as possible. If it sounds right despite the poor reading, I retain it. Otherwise, I try to rephrase it.

A writer may pay too much attention to style. Just as an overdressed person is less elegant than one who dresses in

---

* Wilbur Daniel Steele's short story, "How Beautiful with Shoes."

a casual way, so too deliberate a search for style may result in affectation. And there are other dangers. Virginia Woolf, though a great writer, at times carries her virtuoso style to the point of exhibitionism, as when she follows a very long sentence with an extremely short one. Deliberately? Perhaps not, but one is left in doubt.

Devices such as long blank spaces on the page, oddities in punctuation, strange omissions or ellipses that are supposed to enhance style are pretentious and mannered. Once in a while, certain peculiarities of style are justified. Mark Twain, F. Scott Fitzgerald, J.D. Salinger, and Joan Didion like to italicize not just an entire word but one syllable or even one letter within a word, as in po*lice*, *wor*rying. This isn't a gimmick but an attempt to reproduce more faithfully the way people speak.

A complete inventory of the various styles used in writing is impossible, for there are as many styles as writers. One style, however, though it has many variations, should be mentioned: *stream-of-consciousness* or *interior monologue*. These terms denote the writer's attempt to express the multitude of thoughts, images, and emotions that, like molten lava, are ever in a state of flux in the mind. The writer pours them out, in a disorderly, helterskelter fashion, often ungrammatically, paying little or no heed to punctuation. It is a form of realism, for the mingled thoughts that go on in the mind when the person is not speaking or expressing himself aloud are very much a part of real, subjective life, and there is no reason for a writer to neglect them. For the most famous example, read Molly Bloom's interior monologue at the end of James Joyce's *Ulysses*.

Style, since it is essential to art, is elusive, and it is usually in the heat of the narrative, when the writer thinks of nothing but the scene before him and pays no attention to style, that he achieves the best style. Style is one with inspiration, with a felicitous phrase, with imagination, with rhythm, with full identification with character, object, and situation.

10

LANGUAGE

A S a painter loves color, so a writer loves language. And his ear is attuned to it. The use of precise language, the right word, is proof of that sensitivity, and the appropriate words in a story frequently come naturally, in the first draft, from within. It's interesting how often the first way one writes something is the best.

Here is a passage from one of my stories*:

> Now the peach trees stood, bare of their foliage, in long, stern rows down in the plain, asleep and silent except when the wind blew strong, and then it whistled through them and they seemed to stir. They stood naked, yet so far from dead: each tiny twig intact, waiting and ready—heedful almost.

The words "intact" and "heedful" are especially right and appropriate, I think.

---

* "The Orchard" (*The New Yorker,* June 15, 1968).

There are times, however, when writing is a painstaking, tireless search. A sentence that reads smoothly and seems to have been written easily frequently comes only after many rewritings. In writing my short story "The Secret,"* I spent a long time to produce these opening sentences:

> Like weeds, untended, unintended, needing no extra nourishment or care, their quarrels broke out, flared, and ended, only to rise again more rampant than before. Like weeds spoiling the field, they rose. And he felt that he would have to go.

Particularly in rewriting, in doing second and subsequent drafts, one should keep a dictionary close at hand. Indeed, in the loneliness of creative work, the writer turns to the dictionary as to his only companion, as to an oracle.

Of all authors, Shakespeare uses by far the largest number of different words, but he is the master of conciseness, as in "To be, or not to be." Even James Joyce, with his wealth of made-up and invented words, is a poor second to Shakespeare in the number of different words used. A rich vocabulary alone won't, of course, make a great writer. There are great writers who use a relatively limited number of words.

Using exactly the right word—as, for instance, "stroke" for the flash of the lighthouse lamp in Virginia Woolf's novel *To the Lighthouse*—will be more forceful, more telling, more satisfying for the writer and reader than the approximately right one. Expressing a concept clearly will often

---

* *The New Yorker* (May 7, 1966).

depend on the appropriate word. The thought and the words with which the thought is expressed are intimately connected, and the thought gains vitality and becomes clearer when accurate, precise language is used. That is why a translation will rarely, if ever, have the quality of the original or do more than approximate it. And if you change the order of the words in a fine sentence, something will be lost.

A sentence from Nicholas Delbanco's novel *Sherbrookes* will illustrate this: "When he died of crib death something in her withered that never thereafter could flourish." And the last sentence in Saul Bellow's *Seize the Day* runs: "He heard it and sank deeper than sorrow, through torn sobs and cries toward the consummation of his heart's ultimate need."

A writer should never be reluctant to use simple words just because they are simple. Middle-English words such as "hearty" and "mock" are often more forceful than "cordial" and "imitate," their Latin counterparts. Often simple words have a strength that more unusual ones lack. A writer should not, for instance, look for a synonym for "good" or for "nice" when these words fit the context; to do so would risk being precious. Simple, common adjectives like "bad" and "good" have broad applicability, which may in certain cases be advantageous, but not when a writer wants to pinpoint an idea or description. Thus when wine has a "mellow" flavor, "good" would be too general and imprecise a word to use.

A felicitous expression makes not only for accuracy, but also for conciseness. For example, one might write, "She laughed loud, long and without restraint," or, more suc-

cinctly and just as accurately, "She laughed wantonly."
Again, consider the following:

> She was sitting next to him. After a few minutes she gave
> him a little push with her elbow. "Hi," she said, "don't you
> recognize me?"

"Gave him a little push with her elbow" could be more
briefly and effectively covered by the word "nudged."
Again, instead of "She stood looking at us with her hands
on her hips," we could say with more economy and elegance, "Arms akimbo, she stood looking at us."

Writers are often good listeners: the language they hear
all around them is a fresh spring from which they draw. I
remember a physician using the word "crushing" for the
pain of gout, a plumber using the word "rank" for bad
water, a farmer saying that the wheat was "greening"
when the slopes on which he had sowed it lost their muddy
color and became a delicate green here and there.

Numbers are harder to remember than words. "It was
so cold her hands stuck to the metal of door handles,"
might be more incisive than "It was twenty degrees."
"Stocky" might be better than "Five-foot-two, 160 pounds,
and strong." On the other hand, in describing a Greek
temple, the use of numbers might be most effective, as in "It
looks as though the wind will blow it away, and yet it has
stood there for 2400 years." Here, though the adjectives
"light" and "solid" are not used, the impression of lightness and solidity is conveyed to the reader.

If the writer uses the language that suits the context, he
will give the impression of knowing what he is talking
about, and his story will be more believable, more convinc-

ing. This is especially true if the short story or novel deals with technical matters—ships, business, specific professions, art, law, or whatever. Should a writer be unacquainted with nautical terms and still want to write about ships without doing research, he had better write from the point of view of a passenger rather than, say, the chief engineer.

Writers certainly ought to be encouraged to write about things, people, places, and times they know or have a strong feeling for. Thomas Hardy set his novels in southwestern England, the part he knew best and that he called Wessex. William Faulkner took "a postage-size" part of the world in the Mississippi he knew, called it Yoknapatawpha County, and made it into "a cosmos of [his] own."

As for vulgar words, it is not the words in themselves, but the way they are put together that is sometimes offensive. And at times, the genteel way of saying things is more obscene and indecent than the word or phrase that is reputed to be so. Ann Beattie's short story "Deer Season," for example, hinges on the wording of an insult that one of a group of young people leaves on a deer hunter's car. The note is one that not every magazine would publish, but to change it would reduce the impact of the story. Interestingly enough, though she usually publishes her stories in *The New Yorker*, this one came out in *Canto*.

Often we hear that too many adjectives are used. Generally speaking, I think it is true that the broader the noun, the less it needs an adjective. The word "freedom," for instance, rarely needs to be qualified. On the other hand, a word like "shirt" often requires an adjective.

An apt image, like the right word, livens the writing. The purpose of figurative language—metaphors, similes, comparisons, analogies—is to illustrate, to clarify, to deepen the meaning.

If one likens the lines in an aged face to the wrinkled signature of time, one characterizes the person more accurately and faithfully than if one says that the old face has many lines—an obvious and simplistic description.

To be forceful, valid, and telling, metaphors have to be precise and original. Here are some examples:

> For as we have candles to light the darkness of night, so the cypresses are candles to keep the darkness aflame in the full sunshine. (D.H. Lawrence, in "Twilight in Italy")

Melanie in Thomas Pynchon's novel *V* is described as having eyes "which were the color of freezing rain."

John Updike, in his short story "Separation," compares a man's crying to a wave: "Richard's crying, like a wave that has crashed and crested, had become tumultuous."

When in doubt about the validity of a metaphor or a simile, I try to reverse it to see how it sounds; if it still sounds valid, I keep it. Take this simile from my short story "The Diagnostician"*: "His life—its troubled events, its commotions—was like clouds drifting, merging, blown asunder." The simile when reversed is still meaningful and acceptable. On the other hand, take a poor simile: "Venice is the Disneyland of Europe"; reverse it: "Disneyland is the Venice of America," and its reverse is unacceptable.

---

* *The New Yorker* (December 5, 1970).

To be valid, a figure of speech has to bear a certain measure of truth. "He talked hesitantly and seemed ever in danger of faltering, like a tightrope walker, but like a good tightrope walker, he never did falter, and like one he held our attention." Comparing a person to a machine presents difficulties. As scientists know, a man resembles a daisy far more than he resembles a computer. A unicellular organism is more complex than any machine.

A mixed metaphor is one that contains two or more jarring images, as in the sentence, "The president will put the ship of state on its feet." There is an incongruity in the figure of speech, an incompatibility, that makes the metaphor ridiculous, and *The New Yorker* has fillers with the heading, "Block that metaphor." Sometimes, though the figures jar, the mixed metaphor earns its place through its succinctness and tragic tone: "To take arms against a sea of troubles," or through its comic tone, as in D.H. Lawrence's *Morality of the Novel*: "If you try to nail anything down in the novel, either it kills the novel, or the novel gets up and walks away with the nail."

A number of similes, metaphors, or comparisons in succession can be cloying, but if they are accurate and meaningful, then they are welcome. In my short story "Beppa,"* a paragraph runs:

> As farmers look best in their sun-bleached clothes in the field, coal miners in their black sooty clothes and their boots, fishermen in their heavy sweaters and Levi's, nurses in their white uniforms, and scholars in their shabby attires in the library stacks, so she looked best in her gaudy thin dress at the bar.

* *Antaeus 34* (Summer 1979).

Metaphors may be merely clever: "A balloon is a frus-
trated explosion." Or they may have been clever at one
time but now are no more than clichés: "spaceship earth."

Clichés are second-hand, worn, trite expressions. They
may have had some luster when they were first coined, but
they have been tarnished through overuse. The cliché
"strong as an ox" has at least the merit of being short. A
long cliché such as, "The place was as busy as Grand
Central Station on a Friday afternoon," is more objection-
able, and substituting "Kennedy Airport" for "Grand
Central Station" doesn't make it any better. Similarly,
substituting the word "bull" for the word "ox" in the first
cliché is too easy and obvious a way around the problem
and is probably even worse than using the cliché itself.

A cliché plot is one that follows a formula and leaves
originality no room—bad guy gets killed; virtuous lady gets
married. A cliché characterization is the "stiff-upper-lip
Englishman," the "amorous Frenchman."

When a writer expresses a concept by mentioning or
describing something else—an object, a name—to which
tradition or convention or modern usage or context has
affixed a certain meaning, he is using a symbol: something
concrete is substituted for an abstract object, a lily for
purity, a lion for courage, for instance. There is something
of the cliché in a conventional symbol; it expresses a
thought that has no freshness because it has been said so
often before and has indeed become an accepted, standard
idea. A preconceived, predetermined symbol has a stiff-
ness, a staleness that is the opposite of spontaneity and
originality, and a story that is built around such symbols

risks being stale and hackneyed. Often, too, such a story may be, to the reader, more of a puzzle than a story.

Quite different is the use of symbols that are original, that the writer introduces for the first time and may not be aware of till a critic points them out. The red carnation that Willa Cather has Paul wear in her story "Paul's Case" has been taken by some critics as a symbol of life, and she might have welcomed that interpretation, but I doubt that she saw it as such.

11

PRESENTING THE PAST

M EMORY is our mind's reflection of what happened. When we remember, we transfigure reality; we can't help doing so. Memory is a mirror that time may dim but never dulls. Not a highly polished new mirror whose image will be indistinguishable from objective reality, nor a mirror that distorts, but one on which time has left its mark, and which gives a strange, more poetic, and, in a sense, truer image than the highly polished new one. Not every detail will be shown up; only the most essential, only the most vivid, only the most memorable. Through its selectivity—or, if you will, through the inroads that the process of forgetting will make into it—memory resolves, or goes a long way toward resolving for the artist, the age-old problem of what to put in and what to leave out. And memory presents other advantages, has other qualities. Because it cannot be forced, because it resents any form of compulsion, there is nothing deliberate about it. It is exquisitely spontaneous, beautifully unmechanical. And it has its mystery.

A reflection—a mirror—has in its very nature something artistic. Water, in this sense, was the first artist. Witness the way a neon light reflected on a river loses its artificiality, becomes subjective, is essentialized. Take that red neon sign across the Charles River from my window. It says: "Jordan Marsh Company Fur Storage." It is so objective and hateful and crude if I look at it, and it succeeds so well in peddling its literal, paltry meaning to me. But the moment it is reflected in water, the moment I look at its reflection, I forget all that, and I see only beauty—an extraordinary, liquid, cool, ever-changing, wavering, blending, of red, rose and midnight blue; lights and shadows mingling, reverberating, lengthening, beckoning, crossing over to me. It is matter sublimated, matter transfigured, matter given a soul. It has become form. In the same way, a harsh sound carried along the surface of a body of water will be mellowed by it. The mind, too, may be viewed as a mirror and record of time. Like distance, it lends perspective to the viewer.

"It's autobiographical, isn't it," I'm sometimes asked about a novel or short story of mine, and I detect a note of scorn in the remark, as if autobiographical writing were less imaginative than other fiction writing. But surely this is a narrow view of imagination—unless we regard science fiction as the highest form of literature. Even in science fiction there is much that is autobiographical: to describe the fear, the loneliness, the anxiety of a person lost in space, the science-fiction writer necessarily goes back to his own experiences of fear, loneliness, anxiety, to give a true sense of them to the reader.

Like other kinds of writing reminiscences need to be convincing, unpredictable, and need to have unity, form, a curve. A straight line is unartistic. Often the story will begin and end with the present and the reminiscence itself will be written as a long flashback. Dialogue in it should not be too extensive, detailed and informational, lest the reader ask himself how the narrator can remember so much and his belief in the story be shaken. This is especially true if the reminiscence is set way back in the past. But something of what was said, even a generation ago, usually stands out in the mind of the writer. It may not even be of obvious importance—one of my earliest memories (I was three) is of my father saying, "What a lovely sunset," to my mother. As he writes a reminiscence, the writer will remember things that he thought he had entirely forgotten. The very process of writing will revive certain memories for him. Though truth is the best guide, not everything need be recounted as it actually happened. Certain liberties may be taken, fancy should be given free play. A literal rendition is to be put aside when it works as a stiff scaffolding, and becomes a bond, an impediment. And certain things will have to be changed—the names of the characters, for instance. And the writer himself, if he is in the story, may want to disguise himself, make himself into a painter perhaps. Similarly, the name of a village or of a street may have to be changed. But always an effort should be made to find substitutes that will fit the characters, the places, and the times.

To cite some examples of modern fiction with a strong autobiographical flavor, I might mention Sherwood Anderson's *Winesburg, Ohio*; Bellow's novels *The World of Augie March* and *Herzog*; James Agee's novel *A Death in the Family*; John Updike's collection of short stories, *Problems*;

Bernard Malamud's story collection, *The Magic Barrel*; many short stories by Mavis Gallant and Isaac Bashevis Singer, and Thomas Wolfe's novel *Look Homeward, Angel*.

What is memory? Why do we remember? We remember where our house is so we can find it and go back to it. We remember what happened to us in a certain situation, so that we may avoid or seek again that sort of situation. We remember someone who has died and whom we loved, because it is the thing that will come closest to reviving that person for us. In each case our mind goes back to that place or situation or person in order to renew our knowledge of it.

That is why we remember, to renew the past, and not, primarily, to recount it. And in our fiction writing we must use memory according to its fundamental purpose, its primal cause, its *raison d'être*. When we talk about past times vividly, forcibly, compellingly, and with directness and immediacy, the words we use are not principally a means of recounting those times, but of recalling us to them. We are hardly aware of our audience or of our present selves. We are in the past, where we were. And, for that matter, so is the audience hardly aware of us or of itself. It, too, is in the past, where we have taken it. Or, if you like, the past has become the present. It lives anew.

Were we to tell about the past only to produce an effect on the audience, to instruct them, or to make them aware of it, I am sure the reminiscence would be dull, rhetorical, superficial, and, in the end, ineffective. If we are to be effective in our writing or speaking about the past, we must forget ourselves, our audience, the pen, the paper, the typewriter, the royalty check, the critics, any moralistic urge, no matter how dear to us it may be, and identify wholly with that past—that experience, that person, that situation, that time. This is generally true of all fiction writing, not merely of writing reminiscences. Good fiction writing is a matter of losing one's identity and finding a kinship with the person, place, or situation we are writing about. Otherwise, if we are aware of ourselves and don't identify with the person or situation, we risk being self-conscious writers, and there is no worse kind. The reader then will stop paying attention; he won't be carried away, as the author should have been, by what is being said, but will see the writer as a clumsy performer and dismiss him.

The past is a treasure house of secrets and, if the fiction writer is to be interesting, he must tell them unabashedly. Here again, while he is writing, the writer must forget his readers lest he become self-conscious. In this the writer has an obvious advantage over a speaker, for as a writer writes, the audience exists and doesn't exist; it is a nebulous thing. A speaker addresses himself to one or more listeners; the writer to everyone—and to no one.

When our writing is intimate—inwardly true—then it has universal value, then it is significant, then it is worth telling. Without intimacy, there is no art.

Classifying characters, generalizing about them, ignores their individuality, their innate nature. Even the most nondescript character on the street has a full measure of individuality, if the fiction writer will take the pains to look for it. There are plenty of "plastic characters" in mediocre fiction, but none in real life. There is no art in juggling second-hand ideas, or in the cocksure attitude of those who see no mystery in nature and have a ready-made explanation for everything. There is no art in viewing animals as meat, woods as lumber, scenery as real estate.

Truth and beauty are one. They depend on a strong identification with what is observed and related. Bits of information, factual statements such as saying that the sun rose at 6:17 on a particular day, or that a dear friend has died, though true, have no beauty. But if one identifies with the sun rising or with the death of his friend, then this intimate, deeply felt, cognitive identification *is* beauty, *is* valuable, *is* essential to life and to art. It is one with perception, sensitive apprehension. Without it, even memory, reminiscences, will be robbed of an indispensable constituent, and fall flat. Without it, our memories will be just memories of facts, devoid of feeling, and a sort of inventory of the past, a tedious list, such as none of us would want to live through again or hear about.

12

REJECTIONS AND FLAWS IN FICTION

G REAT novels are often controversial. I recently had to choose seven novels for a course I was teaching. Besides being great novels, one thing they had in common was that for one reason or another they had all had a hard time getting published. They were all turn-of-the-century novels, but in contemporary fiction, too, I can think of many remarkable books that had a difficult start: *Gone with the Wind, Lolita, Catch-22, Ulysses,* and *Lady Chatterley's Lover* are a few that come to mind.

Generally speaking, a collection of short stories is harder to get published than a novel and does not sell as well. Is it because the public finds novels more absorbing and prefers them the way it might prefer a deep sleep to a nap, a full meal to a snack, a long draft to a sip? Or is it that a fine short story—like a fine poem or a drawing—is rarer than a fine novel or painting?

Only if the fiction writer believes in the value of his work can he be persistent enough to keep sending manuscripts

out in the face of the mass rejections he is likely to receive.
The most common reason magazine editors reject short
stories is that they find them too slight. Another common
reason is looseness or lack of unity. The story, they say, is
rambling. Sometimes, in writing a story, the writer uses
too many incidents to illustrate the theme; it is probably
best to concentrate on just one. I once wrote a story that I
called "Bright Spots," about making people laugh, and in
it I related three incidents. Only after I cut two of the three
incidents was the story published, as "The Foghorn."*

At times, aspiring writers (and sometimes established
ones), believing that they must not *state* but only *suggest*,
write stories that are unclear, obscure. They leave out who
said what, and think the reader will understand things that
are not at all clear. Of course there is nothing worse than
stating the *obvious*, but often what the writer is thinking is
far from obvious to the reader. Clarity is the least expendable of the fiction writer's virtues, and although he
should suggest as much as possible, some things need to be
stated. A writer must not follow the advice "Suggest, don't
state" so literally that it comes to mean "State nothing."

A manuscript may be turned down because the writing
is deemed sentimental. This is an ambiguous word and one
that has caused much misunderstanding. As used by most
critics, the word usually refers to writing with excessive or
misplaced emotion. Often affected, it strikes a false note.
The terms maudlin, mawkish, and lachrymose are more
specific and denote an even greater degree of sentimental-
ity as in the following, "The opening of the new recreation

---

* *The New Yorker* (August 2, 1958).

center made the townspeople's hearts tremble with grati-
tude and their eyes shed tears of joyful appreciation.'' Such a
sentence, if it were ever to be published in a story and if it
were to catch a reviewer's attention, would be rightly
criticized as mawkishly sentimental and fulsome. Or, the
following might be criticized as corny: "His eyes watered,
and he reached for a Kleenex as he remembered her sweet,
mellow voice inviting him to her sumptuous southern
mansion—oh my, she was quite a lady!'' The sentence is
in turn maudlin, cloyed with adjectives, and old-fashioned.
It should be pointed out, however, that critics sometimes
use the term *sentimental* to attack a writer's genuine feelings
and the term *realistic* to conceal their own cynicism. To
accept the fake as genuine is a fault, but to reject the
genuine as fake is an even greater fault.

Critics also often inveigh against "self-pity" in judging a
work of fiction. Such criticism is justifiable when a character is shown to feel sorrier for himself than the situation in
a story or novel warrants. But unfortunately, this isn't
what critics usually mean by self-pity; they often label as
"self-pity" what really is sadness, loneliness, despair—
states of mind that have inspired some of fiction's finest
pages, as in Chekhov's story, "The Kiss.''

Lack of freshness is still another cause of rejections. A
subject may have been used many times before in a story,
with more force and originality, and in this instance may
therefore sound too derivative. Didactic, preachy, and
expository writing in fiction accounts for other rejections,
as may faulty technique, clumsy sentences and flashbacks,
stilted dialogue, the use of too many clichés, stereotyped

characters, trite situations and language. But here we are getting into what is simply bad writing.

A writer should try a variety of forms, not just the novel and short story, but also poetry, plays (stage, television and radio), articles, nonfiction books, biography, autobiography, book reviews. One does not always know what one is best at, and often one must count on the reaction of the public.

In writing fiction, there are many ways in which novelists and short story writers can make their work modern and up-to-date. A writer can incorporate into his fiction the latest events, the news, or he may use the latest jargon or even set a new trend in such "true-story novels" as Truman Capote's *In Cold Blood* and Norman Mailer's *The Executioner's Song*. But is this really new? I think that to be new in a creative way and in the best sense of the word is to be original.

When a writer gets stuck and can't go on writing, it is often because the last few words, lines, or paragraphs are wrong. It is well then to go back over them, just as it is advisable to retrace one's steps when one loses the way.

In the face of failure, a writer should not be too disheartened. Aspiration has a way of falling short of achievement, and advances, like the coming of spring, are never steady or continuous; a writer must often take a step back before surging ahead.